The
CIDER
REVIVAL

The CIDER REVIVAL

Dispatches from THE ORCHARD

JASON WILSON

ABRAMS PRESS, NEW YORK

To the apple of my eye

The revolution is not an apple that falls when it is ripe.
You have to make it fall.
—Che Guevara

CONTENTS

CHAPTER 1
CONFESSIONS OF A POMMELIER

As I write this, I am drinking a cider made by a cult producer in New York's Catskills region called Aaron Burr Cidery, named after the treasonous vice president who (as you may have heard) shot and killed Alexander Hamilton in a duel. This particular bottling is labeled Sea Apples, and the apples used to make this cider were hand-foraged from wild, uncultivated trees along the shoreline of remote Isle au Haut off the coast of Maine by the cider makers, Andy Brennan and Polly Giragosian. The trees grow so close to the sea that a light film of salt forms on the apples' skins as they ripen. This bottling was made from fruit harvested during the autumns of 2015 and 2016, and so when I'm drinking it, the cider has a few years of age. It's funky, elemental, mineral, briny. The ripe, earthy apple aromas suggest a gnarled peel, but there are even more far-flung notes that taste closer to old amontillado sherry. Aaron Burr Cidery made only 21 cases of this cider, and it is difficult to find. I've seen it retail at just under $30 for a 500-milliliter bottle, which is smaller than a standard wine bottle. I've seen it on a drinks menu at a fancy restaurant in Manhattan for more than $50.

Suffice to say Aaron Burr Cidery's Sea Apples is about as far from that one, solitary mass-market cider your local craft beer bar probably keeps on tap. If you're like a lot of people, you drank that one cider once and found it sugary, cloying, boring, and something to avoid. You may have never drunk cider again. This is sad, because that's like drinking a glass of Yellow Tail or a cheap boxed wine or maybe even a Bartles & Jaymes wine cooler, and then deciding that all wine—white or red, sparkling or rosé, Old World or New World, grand cru or gluggable—sucks.

These days, in my wine fridge, I have dozens of excellent ciders. They crowd out much of the space that, until recently, was reserved for my favorite wines. I have bubbly ciders and still ciders, tannic ciders and acidic ciders, bone-dry ciders and off-dry ciders, ciders made of American heirloom apples, English bittersharp and bittersweet apples, Spanish apples, French apples, and wild crab apples. Most of these ciders come in 750-milliliter bottles, the standard-sized bottle for wine. Some are made in the same traditional method as Champagne. Others use apples that are macerated with their skins before pressing to achieve an effect similar to red wine. There are bottlings made from a single apple variety, such as 100 percent Northern Spy or Kingston Black or Geneva Tremlett, labeled just like pinot noir or chardonnay or cabernet sauvignon. I even have single-orchard and single-tree bottlings.

Most of the ciders are blends of colorfully named apple varieties: Newtown Pippin, Roxbury Russet, Brown Snout, Golden Russet, Harry Masters Jersey, Ashmead's Kernel, Esopus Spitzenburg, Ellis Bitter, Bulmers Norman, Wickson Crab, Zabergau Reinette—just to name but a few of the hundreds of unfamiliar apples with which one can make cider. Beyond those hundreds are thousands more unnamed varieties growing wild throughout North America, to be discovered by foragers like those at Aaron Burr Cidery. There are about 1,400 known wine grapes in the world—a fraction of the 7,500 apple varieties known to be cultivated. In the US alone there are more than 2,500 identified apple varieties in existence. There have been more than 16,000 varieties cultivated at one time or another in North America, though most of them are now extinct.

All of this may come as a surprise to drinkers who have

experienced cider only through the prism of craft beer, consuming it from that one, sad, lonely tap handle at the bar. But you don't "brew" cider. Cider is essentially apple wine, made with fruit grown in an orchard in the same way wine comes from grapes grown in a vineyard. And like wine, cider can be made only once a year, after the fall harvest. Cider makers even use a version of the truism (or well-worn cliché) that winemakers always repeat: Cider making begins in the orchard. This wine-like approach to cider has recently taken hold so fully that what has evolved is a new species of drinks person termed a *pommelier*, an expert on cider, akin to the sommelier.

Now, if the idea of a pommelier strikes you as utterly absurd, I do not blame you. I once shared your opinion. Only a couple of years ago, the idea of a pommelier existed in the same mental space where I filed other sommelier-wannabes. In my mind, pommelier ranked somewhere below the beer sommelier (or "cicerone"), the bourbon sommelier (or "steward"), or maybe even the cigar sommelier (or "master tobacconist"). Certainly, the pommelier was less ridiculous than the water sommelier, the olive oil sommelier, the tea sommelier, and the mustard sommelier—all of which have also emerged over the past several years. But only slightly.

It's not that I didn't enjoy cider. I secretly loved the good stuff, particularly the complex, dry kind. My skepticism came from my work covering the world of alcoholic beverages. Cider, within this arena, has always been viewed as a second-class tipple. I've written columns on cocktails, spirits, wine, and beer for newspapers and magazines for more than a decade, and only on a few rare occasions have I been permitted by an editor to slip a good word about cider into the mix. I was often trying to advocate for the ciders that I loved, from northern Spain or Normandy or a fine New England producer such as New Hampshire's Farnum Hill. But something was always getting lost in the translation. One of my columns suggested cider as an alternative to wine at Thanksgiving. I still stand solidly by that advice, though I'm pretty sure most readers had not sipped "cider" with their turkey since moving on from the sweet sparkling Martinelli's juice they drank at the kiddie table. For another, even less successful article, I pitched cider as a summer, low-cal alternative to those awful Skinny Margaritas everyone was drinking in the late aughts. You get the picture: Cider always had to be positioned as an alternative to everything else.

Throughout my career, I've turned people on to all manner of obscure and off-the-beaten-path drinks—from bitter amari to strange liqueurs to weird wines made from grapes they can't pronounce from regions they couldn't find on a map. But cider always seemed a bridge too far, a place many simply would not follow. In my personal life, I could feel friends and family wince or glance at one another skeptically, bracing themselves, whenever I opened a cider for them.

The problem was that most people thought of cider as something that existed in a drinks netherworld, that strange sphere where "malternatives" or "alcopops" like Zima, Mike's Hard Lemonade, Twisted Tea, Four Loko, and Smirnoff Ice lurked, a bad crowd up to no good. Cider was something consumed by your gluten-free ex-girlfriend, or that weird ponytailed dude who still played *Magic: The Gathering*, or perhaps out of a jug by some woodsman in Vermont wearing a flannel shirt and a long beard. In fact, it was during my college days in Vermont when I first started seeing so-called "hard ciders" like Woodchuck and Cider Jack pop up next to the IPAs, hefeweizens, and oatmeal stouts.

The biggest issue for cider may be that, for many people, I often still have to clarify that I'm talking about "hard cider," to distinguish it from the apple juice you buy in plastic containers at the farmers market or sugary Mott's or the sparkling Martinelli's of childhood.

Instead, that stuff should be called "soft cider" to differentiate, because the non-alcoholic stuff you drank as a kid is the fake thing. I actually hate when people call cider "hard cider." After all, there is no "hard wine." Wine is to grape juice what cider is to apple juice. Cider is cider—for hundreds of years it's been an alcoholic beverage made from apples and other fruit.

Yes, you'll quickly find that I have strong feelings on cider. That's because somewhere along the journey of my life, I stopped hiding my love of this beverage. A few years ago, all logic be damned, I dove headfirst into the world of cider. Perhaps the bar is low, but at this point I have become—dare I say it—a cider expert. No, probably "expert" is too grand. I don't make cider, and I do not grow apples. No, instead, let's say that I have become a knowledgeable aficionado, an educator, and maybe even a critic. I even passed an exam given by the United States Association of Cider Makers, which bestowed upon me the title of Certified Cider Professional. Dear reader, what I'm trying to say is this: I am now on my way to becoming a Certified Pommelier. God help me. This is my story.

* * *

The first pommelier I ever met was Dan Pucci, a short guy with dark curly hair and a beard who is soft-spoken and usually dressed in a typical white-guy button-down shirt with the sleeves rolled up. This unassuming nature, however, hides a radical fanaticism. Once you get Pucci talking about cider, his blue eyes grow intense and his mouth can barely keep up with the thoughts and ideas spilling out. Pucci becomes a cider evangelist speaking in tongues.

"Cider's issues moving forward are all about expectations and norms," he'd say, as he poured a single-varietal cider from Hereford-shire, England, with a pungent whiff of the cow pasture, or a Basque cider vaguely redolent of balsamic vinegar and berries, or a fleshy, full-bodied, tannic cider called Lost Orchard, made from rare and "feral" apples gathered in Sonoma County by Tilted Shed. "Cider is in a dynamic place right now. People are discovering and rediscovering things. But cider's big challenge moving forward is all about identity. For example, we're not sure if we want to be like beer or wine. We're still figuring shit out in the cider community."

I met Pucci when he worked as cider director of a bar on the Lower East Side of Manhattan called Wassail. Sometimes, I find it hard to believe that Wassail existed at all. It's as if the place were conjured from some cider geek's imagination: an all-cider bar with a vegetarian menu on Orchard Street that took its name from a medieval English Christmastime drinking ritual meant to wake up the apple trees, scare away evil spirits, and ensure next year's bountiful harvest. At Wassail, you would eat dishes made with foraged mushrooms, organic squash, and pickled root vegetables, and concoctions like a salad of cucumber and melon, with macadamia nuts and sorrel leaves, dressed in borage seed oil. Most important, Pucci had curated a list of more than 100 ciders, from all over the world: Normandy and Brittany in France, Asturias in northern Spain, Somerset in the United Kingdom, apflewein from Germany, and elsewhere. More than 20 of them were poured by the glass, and some bottles at the higher end topped $60.

The crowd of drinkers in Wassail was unique. The obvious difference was that it seemed more gender-neutral than other geeky spots for beer or whiskey or mixology. I met people that drank cider because they couldn't drink beer due to a gluten allergy. Some were natural wine lovers who found some of the similar, funky attributes in cider. Others told me they'd started drinking cider because they'd traveled or studied abroad in France or Spain. And others just seemed weird and ultra-retro, like at any moment they might literally stand up and start wassailing. "People who come here don't have preconceived notions about apples or cider. They're open to whatever," said Pucci. "With wine, people come to the bar and say, 'I don't like chardonnay.' No one comes in here and says, 'I don't like Northern Spy or Kingston Black.'"

When the place opened in 2015, critics didn't seem to know what to make of it. "Hanging out at Wassail is like going to a planet populated by nitrogen-based life-forms; everything is at once recognizable and thoroughly different," wrote dining critic Pete Wells, in his review for the *New York Times*. "The proper response," wrote Eater critic Robert Sietsema, "is bewilderment." But even in their bewilderment, they generally gave the place favorable reviews.

Finally, it seemed, cider was having its fashionable turn in the bright pop-cultural lights. "Hard cider is having its craft beer moment," declared *Bon Appétit* in its January 2016 issue. Sales of regional and local craft cider were up 30 percent in 2017, following a 40 percent jump in 2016. The growth was palpable. In 2011 there were 187 registered cideries in the nation. By 2018, there were 820. In 2011, a little less than 5 million people identified themselves as "regular cider drinkers." Only four years later, in 2015, more than 18 million people identified themselves as such. Cider would become a billion-dollar business in 2017. "There's no reason apples shouldn't earn the same respect as grapes," said the drinks site PUNCH in 2016, upon declaring, "Cider is undeniably having a moment in America."

While Wassail's ciders from around the world were wonderful and fascinating, the largest part of the list was given over to American ciders. And while there were a few great ciders from the Pacific Northwest, such as those from Art + Science in Oregon or Snowdrift in Washington, the most essential part of the menu was for ciders from New England and the rest of the northeastern United States. Invariably, my favorite ciders that Pucci poured were from

New York or Vermont or New Hampshire, made with rediscovered, historic cider-apple varieties. As someone who's lived my entire life in the Northeast, including formative years in New England, I felt a deep connection to these beverages. That, to me, felt like the most eye-opening thing about cider. This was more than a "moment" or a passing fad. This was a revival of something that had once been the most important drink in America.

Like me, Pucci had spent many years deep in the wine bubble. He'd trained as a sommelier and sold Italian wine at Eataly and Otto, Mario Batali's casual enoteca. Like me, he was fluent in obscure grape varieties and little-known regions. But he'd grown disenchanted with Italian wine. He grew sick of what he called "fetishizing far-off places" and the "mythology of wine." And so he left wine behind, threw himself into cider, and became a pommelier. One thing that drew Pucci to cider, and keeps him going, is the idea that American cider hails from less exotic origins, places like the Catskills or the Green Mountains, or the Berkshires. As wine critic Jon Bonné wrote in his own profile on Pucci (which also announced "cider's moment"): "You drink wine from Gigondas or Santorini and you're supposedly transported—while cider exudes a sort of comfort in its near-ness."

Cider comes from places where possibly your relatives live, or from the hometown of a friend, or might be where you once went to summer camp or drove through on a family car trip. Or perhaps you've picked fruit at a U-Pick orchard, or bobbed for apples at Halloween, or eaten a candied one on a stick. "I think people, at least here, understand apples in way that we don't understand grapes," Pucci said.

That idea was powerful to me. I'd spent the past three years consumed by writing a book about obscure wines, advocating for little-known and misunderstood grapes like fer servadou, traminer, chasselas, and zierfandler. This took me far from home, wandering around the odd corners of Europe for lengthy periods of time. Back home, I found it difficult to connect with friends and family about my experiences. I'd been off in Europe so much that I also began to feel I was not sufficiently engaged with American topics in a way that seemed critical, especially given the political situation. After I finished writing that wine book, I wanted to reconnect with my own country. In cider's revival, I saw similarities to the cocktail renaissance I'd covered a decade before. The contemporary rediscovery of artisan cider, and the apples to make it, was a sincere attempt to glean the knowledge of an earlier, pre-Prohibition era. It also felt like a chance to revisit a version of rural America that wasn't some dubious, pernicious myth put forth by a red-hatted, orange-faced liar and meant to divide the country.

Then, just as I was about to publish my first article on the American cider revival, suddenly and without warning, at the height of what was supposed to be *cider's moment*—I learned that Wassail might be closing its doors on Orchard Street. At first, there were rumors and speculation. Then Pucci left to start a restaurant consultancy and begin work on an encyclopedic tome about cider. Finally, a few months later, Wassail was shuttered. No reason was given. It's as if the place simply disappeared back into whatever other dimension, whatever alternate reality it had come from.

But by that point, I was in too deep. I felt like someone had to keep talking about the cider revival, and I figured it would be me.

CHAPTER 2
TERROIR & THE NORTHERN SPY

Think about an apple. Try not to think about context and meaning. Don't think about the Garden of Eden or a talking snake who coaxes Eve into eating an apple from the tree of life and all that business about original sin and the so-called "fall of man." (Never mind that the forbidden fruit was probably a fig or a pomegranate anyway.) Forget the golden apples of immortality kept by the Norse goddess Idunn, or the apple that fell on Sir Isaac Newton's head, or the poisoned apple given to Snow White. Forget about an apple a day keeping the doctor away.

Just picture an apple in your mind. If you're like most people, it's a simple thing to conjure, something you've done since childhood—*A*, after all, *is for Apple*. What you're likely imagining is red and shiny and perfectly round. It's the kind of apple you'd find in the grocery store. If we were to put a name to this apple, it might be Red Delicious or McIntosh or Gala or Fuji or Cortland or Jonagold or everyone's new favorite, Honeycrisp. Or perhaps Granny Smith or Golden Delicious if you think in green or yellow rather than red. In any case, you're likely thinking of an apple you can hold in your hand and bite into. These are called dessert apples or culinary apples. They're the sort of familiar fruit that much of the cider in the United States is made from.

Cider from dessert apples veers toward sweet and low in alcohol, with straightforward appley aromas, not too much acidity, and almost no tannins or structure. Ciders like this can be refreshing and quaffable, if they aren't too cloying, which unfortunately many of them are. But they don't offer much in the way of complexity. A cider made from dessert apples is what cider people call *modern*. Modern, in fact, is the official term used by the United States Association of Cider Makers (USACM), a trade group of more than a thousand members, which invested a lot of time and effort in 2017 to create a Style Guide that delineates various categories.

The opposite of modern cider is the other major category—cider made from cider apples. Cider apples are far from the idealized shiny red orbs of childhood. They're often gnarled, rough, russeted, pocked with brown and black spots, oddly shaped, and sometimes the size of little deformed golf balls. These apples might be classified as bittersweets, bittersharps, heirlooms, crab apples, or even wild apples. According to the USACM's Cider Style Guide, ciders made with cider apples are now officially called *heritage*, to differentiate them from modern cider. Heritage cider, the USACM states in its definition, has "increased complexity" and "complex aromatics."

The complexity of heritage cider is created in the orchard. Bittersweet apples like Yarlington Mill, Chisel Jersey, or Dabinett are high in sugar, yet have serious tannins—that drying, black-tea-meets-fuzzy-stone texture that red wine drinkers know well. Meanwhile, bittersharps, such as Kingston Black, Porter's Perfection, and Foxwhelp, pair enamel-peeling acidity with big tannins. Cider apples might have ten times the tannins of dessert apples. Once upon a time, when bittersharps and bittersweets were more common, they were known as "spitters." After I took a particularly astringent bite of a Chisel Jersey at Farnum Hill in New Hampshire, I expectorated and understood why. Farnum Hill's famed orchardist Steve Wood laughed and told me, "You'd be arrested for child abuse if you put that in your kid's lunchbox."

Many of the bittersweets and bittersharps that now grow in North America were first cultivated in England or France, where they have been used for centuries in cider. In Britain, the first references to cider date back to 55 BCE, when the invading Romans observed the Celts fermenting a drink from local apples. More apple varieties were introduced from across the English Channel during the Norman Conquest of 1066. In Normandy, by the 16th century, there were more than 60 named apples officially permitted for cider making. Early settlers brought apples to America, and within a few years after the *Mayflower* landed at Plymouth in 1620, the first apple trees were planted in Massachusetts. By the 1670s, some New England villages were producing more than 500 hogsheads (or 32,000 gallons) per year. By the end of the 18th century, the average Massachusetts resident consumed, annually, about 35 gallons of cider. This was the era of the often-told tale of John Adams' prodigious cider consumption—it's said that Adams drank a tankard every day at breakfast.

Beyond European bittersharps and bittersweets, American heirloom apples are also sought after for heritage cider, bringing complex aromas, minerality, and acidity. Heirlooms such as Northern Spy, Rhode Island Greening, Newtown Pippin, or Golden Russet are historic varieties that were cultivated in early America. The oldest is believed to be the Roxbury Russet, which was first propagated in the 1630s by settlers in the Massachusetts Bay Colony. Many heirlooms were prized for both drinking and eating in centuries past, but at some point they fell out of favor and popular taste, for several reasons. First, there was the emergence of quality beer, brought to America by German immigrants in the mid-19th century, that began to supplant cider as the popular drink. Then, in the early 20th century came the temperance movement and Prohibition, with widely circulated tales of zealots like Carrie Nation chopping or burning down cider orchards. Those stories are mostly apocryphal, but what did change was the perception of the apple—from an ingredient in cider making to something healthy that you ate fresh. The turn of the 20th century was when the marketing slogan "An apple a day keeps the doctor away" became mainstream. By the mid-20th century, the nationwide standardization of fruit for the growing supermarket industry meant relying less on idiosyncratic, local varieties, and more on dessert apples such as Red Delicious, Golden Delicious, Gala, or Granny Smith. In any case, heirloom apples are now kept alive most often in small orchards, coveted by cider makers who blend them with tart crab apples and foraged wild fruit.

Likewise, heritage cider is made mostly by small local producers, people who live in close connection to their apples. On my cider journey, I've focused mainly on this so-called heritage cider and the curious varieties used to make it. Modern cider does not need my help. More than three-quarters of the cider in the United States is produced and sold by large brands such as Angry Orchard, Strongbow, Woodchuck, Crispin, and Stella Artois Cidre, all owned by huge drinks conglomerates. While Angry Orchard does produce a few heritage bottlings, it and the others make predominantly modern cider. No judgment here, and if that's the sort of cider you enjoy, cheers!

My feeling is that if a fermented apple beverage is ultimately going to capture hearts and minds, it will be heritage cider. I'm interested in cider makers who are revivalists, committed to hard work in the orchard, and whose ciders tell the story of a specific place and time. Whose cider have, dare we say it, *terroir*. This wine-like concept makes a lot of cider people, many of whom came to cider via craft beer, very uneasy. "Do apples exhibit terroir, that rather pretentious term applied to wine grapes grown on different soils and in different climates?" asks Ben Watson, in a 2018 essay for the cider zine *Malus*. Watson—who wrote the seminal cider book *Cider, Hard and Sweet* in the 1990s—answers yes to his own question. But note the hand-wringing and characterization of terroir as "rather pretentious."

To be clear, *terroir* is not any more pretentious than other French words you use every day, such as café, salad, omelet, cliché, entrepreneur, encore, fiancé, or toilet. Terroir is simply a fact of agricultural life: better sweet onions come from Vidalia, Georgia, better Ruby Red grapefruit from Texas' Rio Grande Valley, better almonds from California, better maple syrup from Vermont, better lobster from Maine. When I was growing up, I was made to understand that the best tomatoes came from near our home in southern New Jersey.

For cider apples, one of the world's great terroirs happens to exist in a humble, beautiful corner of upstate New York called the Finger Lakes, a cluster of 11 long, narrow lakes about four hours' drive northwest from Manhattan and less than an hour south of Rochester. I already knew that New York was the nation's second-largest apple-producing state. But I'd never tasted a Finger Lakes cider until Dan Pucci poured me several at Wassail, holding forth on the pristine farming practices and old-time apple varieties that abound there. I was immediately blown away by the depth, complexity, and drinkability. These were stunning examples of heritage cider from more than a half-dozen producers. Clearly, some type of cider revival was happening up there. My obsession blossomed, and before I knew it, the Finger Lakes had become almost a second home.

* * *

Wouldn't it have been fascinating to be on the ground in California wine country in the mid-20th century, when winemakers like Robert Mondavi were still just dreaming about American wines becoming embraced by wine connoisseurs? This would have been long before most people had any knowledge of wine geography or vintages or even basic grape varieties like chardonnay or cabernet sauvignon. Think about Napa Valley in, say, the early 1960s, right around the time E&J Gallo introduced its sweet, mass-market Hearty Burgundy wine. The wine world did not take California wine seriously. In the early 1960s, producers like Beringer, Charles Krug, and Ridge were still laboring in relative obscurity, while iconic wineries like Mondavi and Stag's Leap had not yet been founded. By 1972, *Time* magazine was still touting a jug of Gallo's Hearty Burgundy as "the best wine value in the country today." Only a few years later, Napa wines' popularity exploded after the Judgment of Paris, the famed blind tasting when artisan California wines rated above those from Bordeaux and Burgundy.

You hear echoes of Napa's early days in the cider scene around New York's Finger Lakes. The thin isthmus between deep blue Cayuga and Seneca Lakes may have the finest concentration of artisan cideries in the nation. What's emerging is a legitimate cider trail stretching from Ithaca in the south, through the village of Trumansburg, all the way north to Geneva. It's still early, but if I squint into the horizon, I believe I can see it.

I was familiar with the Finger Lakes as a solid cool-climate wine region, renowned for its riesling, cabernet franc, and even blaufränkisch, and I'd spent some time there researching my wine book. I knew day-trippers flocked on sunny days during fall harvest season to taste wine. The lakes, some of the deepest in North America, contribute to a unique microclimate. Since they never freeze, the lakes modulate midwinter temperatures while keeping things cool in the summers. That microclimate is coupled with rich, fertile, well-drained Cazenovia and Honeoye soils, formed from glacial till. This all creates one of the nation's great fruit-growing regions—for grapes *and* apples. Yet terroir is not simply about climate and soil, and that's why it's so often misunderstood. Terroir is also about intangible culture. As I dove deeper, I saw cider treated with a similar respect as the wine.

On a sunny autumn Saturday afternoon at the Finger Lakes Cider House in Interlaken, on a hill with views of Cayuga Lake, I would nudge my way through a boisterous crowd in the tasting room to sample flights of cider. On the deck, a diverse crowd—young and old, straight and gay, white and people of color—snacked on local cheese and charcuterie, picked apples from the orchard, or played cornhole near the barn. "We're proud apple growers and cider makers, just like winemakers who are growers of wine grapes," said Melissa Madden, who with Garrett Miller owns the cider house and farm, along with their cider label Kite & String. One afternoon, while I sampled their Champagne-method ciders, I could see Madden plowing the soil with two horses, in the same old-fashioned way as her Mennonite neighbors. Upon my first visit, I joined the Kite & String cider club just so I'd have a regular reason to return.

Just up the road, at Blackduck Cidery in Ovid, inside a tasting room in a converted barn, iconoclastic and prodigiously bearded John Reynolds pours wild-fermented ciders, riffing on both English and Spanish styles, some a high percentage of bracing crab apples, and some using pears, chokeberries, or currants along with the apples. "People who come here looking for a sweet cider are going to be really disappointed," Reynolds told me. "Our ciders are dry, have a lot of acidity, and they're funky." Yet every time I've tasted there with a crowd, I've seen people happily surprised by the ciders. "Crab apples?" said a middle-aged woman, "Remember when we used to throw them at each other as kids?" "Ohhh," replied her sister. "I actually like these ciders; they're not at all sugary or too appley!"

Just south of the Finger Lakes Cider House and Blackduck, past Bellwether Hard Cider, is downtown Trumansburg, where you'll find plenty of front yards with established apple trees. Here, it's not uncommon to run into cider makers getting coffee, their trucks outside full of the apples they've just harvested from a decades-old home orchard, or foraged from the nearby national forest.

On the outskirts of town sits Black Diamond Farm, where Cornell University emeritus professor Ian Merwin maintains 64 acres with several gorgeous orchards, the first of which he planted in the early 1990s. Black Diamond's apples are both for cider as well as sold as fruit at local farm markets. On special weekends, Merwin might be giving orchard tours and pouring ciders, like his blend of Porter's Perfection, an English bittersharp, and Golden Russet, a New York heirloom originating not far from here in the 18th century. "Cider is the historic beverage in this part of the world," Merwin said. "But in the last 20 years, there's been a tremendous revival." The connection between the Finger Lakes cider community and Cornell University—both its main campus in Ithaca and its experimental agriculture campus in Geneva—is strong, similar to the historic relationship between California wine country and the University of California at Davis.

Each fall, throughout the region, special attention is paid to the apple, New York's leading fruit crop, and to cider. During Finger Lakes Cider Week, restaurants like Hazelnut in Trumansburg or Graft in Watkins Glen will host cider-pairing menus. During Ithaca's apple harvest festival, in the wineshops downtown, you're just as likely to find a cider tasting. For instance, at Red Feet Wine Market, near the Ithaca Farmers Market, I attended a presentation on "Finger Lakes Cider in International Context" with comparative tastings between local ciders and those from the Basque Country, Normandy, and the Alps. That presentation was given by a cider maker named Autumn Stoscheck, who's been making her Eve's Cider here for two decades. If we're keeping with our Napa Valley metaphor, Autumn Stoscheck would be the Robert Mondavi character in the Finger Lakes cider story. Thirty people crowded into the store to taste, as Autumn told them stories about centuries and decades past in the Finger Lakes, when cider mills abounded. She asked the crowd, "Why did we forget about cider?"

*　*　*

"Can you taste a place?" asked Autumn, as she poured several ciders made from her Northern Spy apples. "I think you can."

This was my first visit to Eve's Cidery, at the far southern end of the Finger Lakes region, a little southeast from more touristed towns like Watkins Glen or Hammondsport. To get to Eve's, you drive through Van Etten, a gritty village of about 1,500 people with a mini-mart, a post office, a hair salon, McCann's Restaurant & Liquor, and not much else. You take a winding road over a narrow bridge until you arrive at a barn adorned with a large photograph of the same barn (some kind of unexplained art project). The cidery is in the barn, next to a modest farmhouse with chickens and dogs roaming outside. It was a cold late morning, and I was sitting at the farmhouse table, amid rustic-hippy, harvest-season chaos. Autumn poured the Northern Spy ciders in between making a salad of celery root and red cabbage, putting a veggie frittata in the oven for lunch, and looking at drawings and stories by her homeschooled children, Leila, 11, and Zuri, eight. "They're very artistic," she said. "They can learn in one hour what it takes kids in the public school eight hours to learn."

Yes, Autumn is the perfect name for a cider maker and orchardist, and she exudes the gentle, soulful ideal of a benevolent, radiant apple goddess, one who is revered in cider circles. Everyone knows her on a first-name basis, simply as Autumn. "She holds the truth," I was told by a young, up-and-coming Finger Lakes cider maker, one of many who count her as a mentor.

Still, don't be fooled by the easygoing, Earth Mother vibe. Autumn is intense about the art of cider making and does not suffer fools, talking forcefully against what she sees as "cheap, sweet junk" in "skinny cans and craft beer packaging" that mostly passes for cider in the marketplace. "They're just making up a beverage and co-opting words and ideas from traditional cider in order to sell alcoholic soda," she said, albeit with a warm smile, as she served me a delicious triangle of frittata. She poured her husband and partner, Ezra Sherman, a bowl of bone broth since he had just been diagnosed with a stomach condition and they were intent on healing him through a natural, healthy diet rather than prescription medicine or surgery. A poster next to the light switch in the bathroom declares, "Capitalism Is a Pyramid Scheme."

When Autumn was 19, in the late 1990s, she'd taken a "leave of absence" from Cornell and was waitressing and working in an apple orchard. "That's when I learned to prune apple trees and at that time, I felt as if I had discovered the meaning of life," she said. One day, she read an article in *Fruit Grower News* about an orchardist in New Hampshire named Steve Wood, who was growing cider apples and pressing them into artisan cider. She was transfixed and drove five hours to meet Wood, showing up unannounced at his Poverty Lane Orchards. After Autumn asked dozens of questions and gathered all the wisdom and knowledge she could, Wood gave her cuttings of young shoots from his various cider apple trees. These twigs with fresh buds are called scion or budwood, and grafting them onto existing rootstock—literally joining together the vascular tissue of scion and rootstock—is the only way to propagate specific apple varieties from one orchard to another. Once Autumn returned to the Finger Lakes with the scion wood from Poverty Lane Orchards, she took all her savings from waitressing and grafted her first trees, with the help of a local, sixth-generation orchardist named James Cummins.

By 2002, she'd bottled her first ciders, which she and Ezra sold at the Union Square farmers market in Manhattan, sleeping overnight in their van. "This is such a long project," she said. "I'm now almost 40 and we're still just beginning."

We tasted three of her single-varietal Northern Spy bottlings, each from a different harvest from 2014 through 2016. These were intense, nervy ciders with soaring acidity, almost like a great, unaged riesling or like many of the natural wines that younger drinkers have fallen for. At that point, I'd tasted a few all-Northern-Spy ciders, but never a vertical tasting of the variety over several years. "We love this apple," she said. "And we're just getting to the point where we're starting to understand it."

The Northern Spy bottlings had been produced using the same traditional method as Champagne, with the cider aging in the bottle on the lees, the leftover yeast particles that remain as sediment after fermentation. In the 2014 "vintage," the acidity had mellowed enough that complex, secondary aromas of sea salt and wet stones emerged. The 2015 "vintage" was full of apple strudel aromas and big tannins, while the 2016 was juicier and even more tannic, with bright notes of citrus along with a long finish with the bite of the apple's peel. I use *vintage* in quotes because the government does not allow ciders to be labeled with a vintage year. Part of this is because an apple harvest year would technically not be a vintage, which refers to wine grapes (*pommage* might be more accurate). But cider makers believe the policy has been unduly influenced by the wine industry to deny cider the same prestige as wine. In response, many ciders work around the label restrictions with "lot numbers" (Lot #16 to denote 2016, for instance) so that drinkers are clued in to the harvest year.

The Northern Spy apple was discovered in East Bloomfield, New York, just south of Rochester, about two centuries ago. It's believed that the name was taken from a popular pulp novel of the 1830s,

The Northern Spy; or The Fatal Papers, a Tale of South Carolina, in which the hero, an abolitionist spy, infiltrates a group of Southern slave catchers. The name is apt, since this part of New York was connected to the Underground Railroad—Harriet Tubman and Frederick Douglass both lived in the Finger Lakes. "I think it's good to have an apple that reminds us of this history," Autumn said.

Once upon a time, the yellow-and-red-streaked Northern Spy was among the most popular apples in the Northeast for eating and cooking. By now, though, Northern Spy has mostly been phased out in favor of more modern apples, which are bred for disease resistance and tested in a lab to look prettier and more uniform in the supermarket, to fit a consumer taste profile, and even to crunch in a specific way when bitten. To a cider maker, however, the only thing that matters is the flavor and texture that's unlocked by fermentation. Autumn told me that growing this fruit organically in her orchards costs four times what it would cost a large commercial orchard that would use chemically intense farm practices. In total, Eve's tends to around 5,000 trees, with about half of those old enough to bear fruit right now, ranging from eight to 40 years old.

After lunch, we both put on heavy coats, hats, and gloves and hiked up a seasonal-use dirt road closed in colder months ("Travel At Your Own Risk" read the sign) to the Albee Hill orchard, essentially Eve's grand cru. The orchard sits about 1,000 feet above sea level. She pointed toward the mountains to the south. "We're really as much at the end of the Appalachians here as we are in the Finger Lakes. This soil was all created by a prehistoric glacier. This is one of the greatest places for growing fruit in the world."

Albee Hill's soil is pure shale, which is similar to the soil where excellent riesling grows in prestige regions of Germany. The shale stresses the apple trees. "I believe apples are similar to grapes," Autumn said. "You get better apples when the trees have to suffer.

In rich, lush soil, you get big, pithy apples, which isn't what we want for cider. I want tension, struggle, maturity." There is Northern Spy here, along with about 40 other apples varieties, including Idared, Bramley's Seedling, Dabinett, Cox's Orange Pippin, and Golden Russet—another classic New York apple discovered in the early 19th century not too long after Northern Spy. The complex blend Autumn makes from this orchard is dry and still, with no bubbles. It's as serious and deep as cider gets, with dark fruit, stony minerality, and austere tannins. Every year, it's a classic. People unfamiliar with good cider don't immediately know what to make of it.

The sun began to set and the cold wind picked up as we hiked down Albee Hill, this time through the woods back to the farmhouse. As we walked, Autumn told me she'd be taking a sabbatical the next year to work with a nearby riesling producer and also planned to work a wine harvest in the Rhône Valley in the fall—she wanted to see what a cider orchardist could learn from winegrowers. Ezra would take the lead role in the orchard and the cidery. She admitted to feeling a little burned out after this harvest, and that she was recovering from the Lyme disease she got the previous summer. She also said that the news of Wassail closing had been a "gut punch," especially to New York cider makers. "I honestly worry about the longevity of cider," she said. "In 2013, we were like, 'Oh my god, cider is blowing up.' But we still have a long way to go to build a solid market. For the larger category to have depth, cider makers, and cider drinkers, are eventually going to have to care about the cider fruit."

* * *

Terroir is never just about one person, and so I also spent a good deal of time with up-and-coming cider makers who followed Autumn's trailblazing in the Finger Lakes. I can pinpoint two Finger Lakes ciders, which I first tasted at Wassail, that completely transformed my idea of what fermented apple juice could be: South Hill's Packbasket, made with 100 percent wild-foraged apples, and Redbyrd's Andromeda Crab, which had structure almost like a red wine. On my first cider trip to the Finger Lakes, I met Steve Selin of South Hill and Eric Shatt of Redbyrd at a wineshop in Ithaca called Cellar d'Or, where they poured bottles during the apple harvest festival.

Selin and Shatt are soft-spoken, genuinely nice guys who had been influenced by, among others, Eve's Cidery. Per Autumn's dictum, they cared deeply about the cider fruit. Both wore flannel shirts and their hair pulled into long ponytails flecked with gray—as time went on, I would come to recognize the flannel and ponytail as essential to the male cider maker's uniform. Shatt started selling cider to the public in 2010 and Selin in 2014, though both made cider at home for more than a decade before that.

That week, Shatt invited me to his home, a few miles from Trumansburg, where in 2011, he planted a five-acre orchard with his wife, Deva Maas, and their three boys. For his day job, the 41-year-old manages Cornell University's research orchards, and he previously worked as a winemaker. "I'm most interested in expressing the terroir and focusing on the fruit," Shatt said. "As cider makers here in the Finger Lakes, we're more influenced by wine than we think. We have an acceptance of acidity, for instance. We like acidity."

At the moment, Shatt makes less than 2,000 gallons of cider, including kegs, and about 800 cases per year, with a limited supply of his premium bottlings with names like Cloudsplitter and Starblossom. Shatt uses Champagne yeast and makes several of his ciders, such as his Celeste Sur Lie, in the traditional Champagne method, with a second fermentation in the bottle, and aging on the lees for months or years before disgorging. "I love what this technique does for cider," he said. Another thing that sets Shatt's premium bottles apart is that they push the needle when it comes to alcohol by volume, with most of them above eight percent. Redbyrd's Andromeda Crab is actually above nine percent alcohol by volume, which is about a third more than most mass-market ciders, and nearly the same level as some wine, such as riesling from Mosel, Germany.

Shatt and I walked into his biodynamic orchard, planted with about 2,000 trees—though many are still too young to bear fruit for cider. "We want maximum intensity of flavor," Shatt said. "I prefer picking apples off the ground. If you wait until they fall to the ground, they'll come to full ripeness." Orchardists are permitted to do this with apples meant to be fermented into cider, but not for sweet non-alcoholic cider due to contamination risks.

"Apples should have tannins and acidity," he said, as we continued along the rows. "They've bred that out of them just to create these big red sugar balls for the supermarket." With about 100 varieties, Shatt grows many of the same bittersharps, bittersweets, and heirlooms as those at Eve's or Black Diamond, including Northern Spy. But he has several unique apples that no one else possesses.

As we wandered, Shatt stopped and grabbed a large yellow-green and orange-blushed apple and handed it to me. "I discovered this apple in the wild," he said. "The tree in the wild had been naturally pruned by a deer"—a phenomenon, he said, that foresters call "deer browsing." Clearly the deer found this apple delicious and wanted it to survive. Shatt had cut branches from the original wild tree and grafted them to rootstock in his own orchard to cultivate the wild variety. This act, to domesticate the wild apple, was the embodiment of what Michael Pollan writes in his book *The Botany of Desire*: An orchard has always been "an idealized or domesticated version of a forest, and the transformation of a shadowy tract of wilderness into a tidy geometry of apple trees offered a viable, even stirring, proof that a pioneer had mastered the primordial forest."

After I'd taken a few bites of the orange-blushed apple, Shatt said: "I named it. Gnarled Chapman. It's a reference to Johnny Appleseed."

With the mention of Johnny Appleseed—an American legend, as well as an actual early 19th-century nurseryman named John Chapman—I was suddenly transported far away from Trumansburg. A bite of this Gnarled Chapman apple took me back more than 200 years, to when Chapman spread apple seeds throughout Pennsylvania and the newly acquired Northwest Territories, which would eventually become Ohio, West Virginia, Illinois, and Indiana. We learn the story of Johnny Appleseed when we're in grade school, where he is held up as a benevolent wanderer, a symbol of taming the American frontier, dressed in a burlap sack with a tin pot for a hat—a guy who freed a wolf from a trap and kept it as a pet. But the real, historical John Chapman was a more complicated figure. He was a savvy businessman who planted prosperous nurseries and acquired 1,200 acres of land by his death in 1845. Chapman was a vegetarian who hiked barefoot, as well as a Christian missionary who preached his gospel to Native Americans, converting many of them. He was steeped in Swedenborgian religious philosophy, the teachings of the Swedish theologian Emanuel Swedenborg, who believed in "correspondences" between the natural and spiritual worlds, as close to nature worship as Christianity ever gets. Yet it's important to remember, and nearly all historians agree on this: The apples trees Chapman planted were not for eating or cooking. Like most apples grown in the early 19th century, they were to be used in the cider barrel. Pollan calls him "the American Dionysus," which makes a lot of sense. It's hard for us now to imagine just how important cider was to early America—a place where fermented apple juice was safer than water, and even children consumed it daily.

The Gnarled Chapman variety is not the only one that Shatt has domesticated from a wild seedling. There's also Searsburg Cherry

Bomb, which he found growing along nearby Searsburg Road. "And it looks like a cherry bomb!" he said. Biting into the tiny Searsburg Cherry Bomb, the taste was a crazy explosion of tropical fruit, almost like lychee. A few rows down was Barn Hill Sharp, a crab apple he found on a tree growing out from the stone foundation of an old barn. He handed me the tiny crab and said, "This is the sharpest apple you will ever eat." It was like biting into a Meyer lemon, and my mouth puckered. It was a true spitter.

I enjoyed thinking about Shatt as a sort of modern-day Johnny Appleseed. In fact, he's been generously open-sourced with the apples he's discovered, sharing them freely with other orchardists and even giving them to nurseries in the Finger Lakes as well as ones with nationwide mail-order reach. Fedco Trees in Maine now lists Gnarled Chapman in its eagerly awaited annual tree catalog as "Recommended for trial in all cider-apple growing districts." Maybe years from now, we'll know Gnarled Chapman in the same way cider geeks now know Northern Spy.

* * *

By the time I visited Steve Selin one afternoon a few days later, I'd begun wearing flannel shirts, muddy boots, and a baseball cap every day. When I met Selin at his cidery, he was unloading a pickup truck full of apples in wooden crates. Normally, as a journalist, I would just stand there as an observer, notebook open and pen at the ready, asking questions while staring awkwardly at this guy as he unloaded stacks of heavy crates. On that day, however, I was so wrapped up in the moment, of my new love of apples and cider and the Finger Lakes, that I just jumped in and unloaded the truck with him—journalistic neutrality be damned.

Before Selin became a cider maker, the 45-year-old worked as a luthier, making violins. This interested me because I'd once lived in the world's mecca of violinmaking, Cremona, Italy—the home of Stradivarius, Guarneri, and other 16th- and 17th-century master luthiers. In Cremona, there is still a famous violin school, museum, dozens of artisans, and its luthier tradition is actually protected by UNESCO as "intangible cultural heritage." "In Cremona, they were able to elevate the craft of violinmaking because all the great crafts-men were there," Selin said. "With cider making, we have a commu-nity in the Finger Lakes that's similar to what they had in Cremona. That was the concept that gave me the confidence to switch careers and jump into cider making."

Selin began making cider at home in 2003, but it wasn't until 2013 that he got his New York State farm cidery license, and he started selling to the public the following year. Now he produces around 4,000 gallons per year, with a good portion sold in kegs to bars and restaurants, and about 1,000 cases of bottles. He's planted his own orchard, with about 1,500 trees, next to his home on the South Hill of Ithaca, at an elevation of 1,100 feet above sea level. He also has relationships with home orchardists throughout the region to harvest their apples. That's what he does with his single-orchard Stone Fence Farm bottling, made of fruit from the farm of his neigh-bor Peter Hoover, a local aficionado and amateur distiller who trades him apples for cider. Just like several others in the region, Selin also makes cider from foraged wild fruit.

In fact, on that day, Selin drove me to one of his secret forag-ing locations in the Finger Lakes National Forest to show me the trees he'd soon harvest to make Packbasket, the cider I'd first tasted at Wassail. As we drove into the forest, Selin suddenly slammed on the brakes. "Are those apples or pears?" he exclaimed, jumping out of the cab to grab one. After a bite, he told me it was too softly sweet and low acid for cider, then chucked it. Finally, Selin parked his truck in a clearing off the road. He grabbed a bottle of Packbasket, some glasses, and we hopped the fence. "This is the fun part of the job," he said. Though he added: "It's hunting season, and so I usually run into guys with guns out here. Also, I'm not sure if I'm supposed to get a permit or not."

We wandered out into a meadow, where several dozen cows grazed, the entire area ringed by dozens of apple trees. Throughout the 19th century, this part of the National Forest had actually been inhabited by farms. During the Depression, the federal government acquired this land, relocated all the residents, and the area was abandoned. Yet since nearly every homestead in the 18th and 19th centuries had an orchard, and the apple trees here are both artifacts and offspring of those old orchards, this area is a living monument to how important the apple once was. Cows have continued to graze the land since that time, eating wild apples that fall to the ground. After the cows poop, many of those undigested apple seeds become trees, and after many more years, the seedlings that survive and become established begin to bear fruit unlike anything you can grow in an orchard.

Apples, similar to humans, are heterozygous. That means that they produce offspring that are unique from their parents. Every seed inside every apple has different genetic content, and each seed will grow a completely new variety of apple, distinctly different from its parents. Even if you took a seed from the supermarket apple you ate for lunch and planted it, a brand-new, never-seen-before seedling would grow. That's why the only way an orchardist can cultivate the same apple over and over again is to graft the scion wood from that variety onto existing rootstock. That's also why there are thousands of unknown apples growing in the wild. All the apples Selin and I scouted that afternoon were as-yet-unnamed varieties. "It changes every year, which trees blossom and which ones don't," Selin said. "There's such an overabundance of wild fruit around here. I know 10 times the amount of trees I can harvest."

As we moved from tree to tree, a few cows followed us. "Here are the girls," Selin said, tossing them a few apples. More cows followed. We came upon a tall, thick tree with tons of tiny brown golf-ball-sized apples. "Oh, yeah! Here we go! This is one of my favorite trees. These are little russets," Selin said, taking a bite and passing it to me. "Oh my god, these are going to be great in the next couple weeks." He hadn't brought his refractometer, but he estimated that these apples had "at least 19 brix of sugar," which was high for apples and would ferment well into alcohol. They also had great tannins and acidity.

By the time we turned around again, about forty cows had lined up behind us waiting for apples. We tossed a few and retreated to another tree a few hundred yards away. We sat on a stone, likely an old foundation of an abandoned farmhouse. Selin opened the bottle of Packbasket 2015 and poured cider into the glasses. The cider was bone-dry, with razor-like acidity, and full of complex flavors—old stone, wildflowers, grass, autumn leaves, even a tiny bit of cow-pasture funk, but balanced by bright, fresh fruitiness. It was undeniably a taste of this place.

I was beginning to feel very much at home among apple trees on sunny fall afternoons. It all felt so different from the many, many vineyard tours I'd been part of. By comparison, the rows of apple trees felt restorative, even hauntingly familiar. Amid the hunt to rediscover heirloom apples, and domesticated wild apples, and feral apples, I was beginning to feel like I was a part of recovering something American that had been lost.

CHAPTER 3
WALDEN TO WURTSBORO

Amid my starry-eyed reverie about heritage cider and lost apples, I realized, of course, that there's also nothing more American than turning a quick buck. That's why, on a few occasions, I traveled three hours south from the Finger Lakes to the Hudson Valley, the Apple Belt of New York. My destination was Angry Orchard's Innovation Cider House, in the town of Walden.

Even people who don't know anything about cider know Angry Orchard. You've seen the television commercials, you've seen the bottles in your beer-store fridge next to the Bud, Coors, and Miller Lite, you've seen the rosé cider. Angry Orchard is so ubiquitous that sometimes it's surprising to remember the brand was only launched in 2011 by Boston Beer Company, which owns Sam Adams. It was an immediate success, driving the entire cider industry to grow by 65 percent in 2012, then double again by 2014. By 2015, Angry Orchard was selling about 15 million cases per year—more than seven times its nearest competitor, Woodchuck. There's no doubt that Angry Orchard is single-handedly responsible for cider's visibility and mainstream appeal. It now controls roughly 60 percent of the total cider market in the United States. Angry Orchard is the definition of Big Cider.

In my travels, I heard a lot of rancor over Big Cider from smaller producers. "Angry Orchard defines the problem," Autumn Stoscheck of Eve's Cidery had told me, referring to its mass-market ciders as "obvious junk." For these cider makers, the biggest issue was Angry

Orchard's source of fruit for most of its bestselling ciders: apple juice concentrate. This is common for many large corporate producers, some even getting cheap concentrate from China—where the price is "virtually negligible," according to some in the industry. Angry Orchard, however, says that its concentrate has always come from Europe and that there's invariably a percentage of bittersweet cider varieties in the juice. Additionally, in 2015, Angry Orchard opened the Innovation Cider House, on a 60-acre apple orchard in Walden, where the cider makers could do research and development and experiment with special, limited-edition ciders.

The first time I arrived at the Innovation Cider House, on a mid-fall Wednesday, the entire parking lot was full. I had to park in "additional parking," near rows of trees laden with nearly ripe apples. A sign next to the lot warned: "Don't make our trees angry by picking the apples. That's our job."

When I entered the big red barn-like Cider House, I was fitted with a bright orange wristband, signifying that I was indeed over 21. I wandered the self-guided museum tour, looking at circa-1960s orchard equipment used by the family who'd owned this farm before Angry Orchard bought it. A sign says that the old wooden sorter "used to expedite the process of separating good and bad apples" and a worn ladder bears a placard that reads: "Ladders have always been essential to pick fruit in the fall and prune branches in the winter." I flipped through a booklet of Angry Orchard–approved cocktails, such as Angry Balls: an ounce and a half of Fireball added to a glass of Angry Orchard Crisp Apple Cider, over ice.

I took a few moments to read the illuminated time line of apple and cider history, from the first cave paintings of apples in 8000 BCE to the first documented apple sale on a Mesopotamian tablet in 1500 BC, to Egyptian pharaoh Ramses the Great planting orchards along the Nile, to settler William Blackstone planting the first orchard in

Boston in 1625. There was, of course, the obligatory mention of John Adams and his daily tankard. I love the history of apples, because it essentially mirrors human history. The apple originated thousands of years ago in Central Asia, in the mountains of Kazakhstan, according to DNA analysis. There, wild *Malus sieversii*, the ancestor of our domesticated *Malus domestica*, still grows in abundance. The apple made its way to Europe in 328 BCE when Alexander the Great conquered Persia and discovered the native Kazakh rootstock and grafting techniques, which he took home to Greece. This history lesson I was following at Innovation Cider House led to a few self-serving milestones along the illuminated time line. Following Prohibition, the time line jumped all the way to 1995, when "Angry Orchard cider makers began experimenting with hard cider!" followed by 2011, when the company released its ciders, and ending at 2015 with the Innovation Cider House itself opening to the public.

After the tour, I browsed the gift shop, where one could buy Angry Orchard–branded flannel shirts, work jackets, and T-shirts that read "Barrel Aged." Finally, I went to the pouring station for my tasting flight of three ciders. "The ones on the left are sweet and the ones on the right are dry," said the young woman behind the bar, after she asked to see my wristband. I steered away from the obviously sweet, and ordered Understood in Motion #2 (a collaboration with E.Z. Orchards in Oregon), a ginger-flavored cider (with "ginger sourced from the Hudson Valley"), and Walden Hollow—which was Angry Orchard's first cider made entirely from New York State apples. I'd been told by insiders that Walden Hollow was Angry Orchards' first mass-market cider that did not use concentrate.

I carried my flight over to a long table in the bright, bustling tasting room. Most of the tables were full, so I sat next to a birthday party of college-aged kids, all playing the classic board game *Operation* while they drank cider. "Funny bone for $800!" one shouted.

The father of the birthday boy asked the group if they wanted to take a tour. "Am I allowed?" asked one young woman, who did not have a wristband. The ones who did have wristbands ordered another round. *Bzzzzzzzz*, sounded *Operation* after someone was unsuccessful at removing the bread basket for $1000.

The father, an affable guy who lived nearby in the Hudson Valley, struck up a conversation with me. He was sipping a pint of Gin Botanical, a cider flavored to taste like gin. He suggested that I try the Autumn Farm Cider, which he described as sort of like the Walden Hollow, "but sweeter." We talked about his recent trip to Napa Valley with his wife, and he compared the place to the winery tasting room experience. "There was such a focus on all the different kinds of grapes," he said. He raised his glass of gin-flavored cider. "I wonder what kind of apples they use in this?"

* * *

I returned to the Innovation Cider House a few weeks later, to talk with head cider maker Ryan Burk. We met after the tasting room's closing time, just as it was getting dark on a nippy fall evening. Burk had just returned from yet another trip into the market as the face of Angry Orchard. I told him the now-empty tasting room was quite different from my last visit. "Yeah, we're seeing 3,000 people in here on a Saturday," he said. "It's been a huge success."

You might have seen Burk in Angry Orchard's most recent commercials, wandering the orchard and cidery amid guitar riffs and cinematic jump cuts reminiscent of a 1990s music video. In those spots, Burk sits in the sun with a bottle of cider, tattoo poking out from under his T-shirt sleeve, talking about how "some of the ugliest, angriest apples make the best cider." He tells the television audience, possibly watching a Sunday NFL game, that "bittersweet apples have tannin" and that "At Angry Orchard, we're using tannin to make a cider that's complex and interesting."

In person, the 38-year-old actually resembles an aging grunge rocker: knit beanie pulled tight; shaggy beard beginning to gray at the edges; chest tattoo peeking out from the V in his button-down shirt. It makes sense to learn that he played in hardcore bands in Rochester in his 20s. Burk grew up in Williamson, New York, in Wayne County, north of the Finger Lakes, near Lake Ontario. Almost half of Wayne County's 600 square miles is farmland, mostly apple farms. Williamson's town motto: "The Core of Apple Country." Growing up, Burk and his friends were well acquainted with making and drinking clandestine cider. "I wouldn't want to give anyone's secrets away. But you could certainly find barrels of ciders fermenting in people's cellars," he once told his hometown newspaper, the *Rochester Democrat & Chronicle.*

Burk was clearly tired from his travel and seemed a little defensive. One of the first things he told me was, "You can hate on Angry Orchard until you're blue in the face. But we're a good company that cares about quality, and cares about apples and cider making."

The first thing he poured me was Understood in Motion #2, his collaboration with E.Z. Orchards in Oregon. Other collaborations in this series have been with other highly regarded cider makers such as Eleanor Léger from Eden in Vermont, and Tom Oliver, a UK producer beloved by cider geeks. Understood in Motion #2 is a solid cider, with some tannins and a little bit of acidity, though still veering toward off-dry—a cut above Angry Orchard's mass-market bottlings. It's the kind of cider one hopes might nudge a committed Angry Orchard drinker toward something slightly drier and more complex. I asked Burk if we'd see Understood in Motion in retail stores next to the usual bottles of Crisp Apple and Easy Apple. "No," he said. "This is only going to curated places. Places that I trust will tell the right story."

He then poured me single-varietal bottlings made with Baldwin and Newtown Pippin—both also solid and drinkable, but again, very limited edition. We wandered through the Cider House and into a room, where we tasted a Spanish-inspired cider from the barrel. As we sipped, he told me that Angry Orchard's small-batch ciders had won all sorts of international awards earlier that year. "Not to gloat, but we had a pretty good year," he said, finally smiling. "I know that irritates a lot of the smaller guys."

Before he came to Angry Orchard, Burk had been in law school in Chicago, where he became active in the home brewing scene. Eventually he scrapped the law and went to work for Virtue Cider in Michigan, just as it was being launched by the former brewmaster of Goose Island. Burk spent four years at Virtue, before it eventually was acquired by Anheuser-Busch InBev. In 2015, Angry Orchard hired him to open its Innovation Cider House, as well as manage what he calls "the national program"—the 30 million gallons of mainstream Angry Orchard product that most consumers encounter. Those mass-market ciders are mostly made at separate facilities in Cincinnati and Allentown, Pennsylvania.

But the Innovation Cider House is where Burk can experiment and make what he likes. In Walden, he's making only 40,000 gallons of cider annually, about 17,000 cases—most of which will go only to the "curated places" that he trusts "to tell the right story." Walden's production may be a drop in the bucket for Angry Orchard, but consider that it's about six times what Eve's Cidery produces, ten times what South Hill makes, and 20 times that of Redbyrd.

"Everything we're doing here is dry," Burk told me as we tasted.

"What about the national ciders?" I asked.

"I can't comment on that," he said, with a laugh. "What we do here, that they don't necessarily do on the national level, is to focus on dry."

As we toured and tasted among the barrels of Burk's experiments, it was clear to me that he understood better than anyone where cider seemed to be headed. "There is a trend toward drier. Mouthfeel, tannin, body. We as a cider industry need more of that thing," he said. "I don't believe that beer-making-style ciders, like a gose cider or a dry-hopped cider, is the future. I believe the future of our industry is the apple. Apples are what we should be focused on."

I appreciated that sentiment, but I expressed my skepticism. It seemed a little cynical now, after a half decade of selling people on sweet and simple modern cider from concentrate, that Angry Orchard would make a small pivot to the heritage, orchard-based side. It also seemed possibly misguided. After all, Angry Orchard had already turned so many potential cider drinkers on to sweet, simple, and cheap. Now the company would convert them to dry and complex? There is an attractive theory in the drinks industry—the gateway theory—that if you recruit new drinkers to something simple, sweet, and cheap that they will eventually evolve, developing a taste for the sophisticated, high-end: The Yellow Tail chardonnay drinker will eventually crave grand cru Burgundy; the lover of black-cherry- or honey-flavored Jim Beam will eventually seek out single-barrel, cask-strength bourbon. Large beverage companies love to trot out the gateway theory as an excuse to sell mediocre or poor products alongside a few legitimately good ones. But there is almost no evidence to show that this gateway theory works; in fact, most people—once hooked by marketing and availability—stick with what is simple, sweet, and cheap.

But maybe I'm the cynical one. Among cider people, there's been praise for what Burk is trying to do at the Innovation Cider

House. In the cider zine *Malus*, author Darlene Hayes wrote an essay titled, "Don't Be Angry: Give Ryan Burk a Break," in which she asks, "Is Big Cider trying to pull a fast one on discerning cider makers and consumers alike?" Her answer is a cautiously optimistic "no." Though acknowledging that Angry Orchard is "an obvious target of mistrust," she points out the company's transparency, its efforts to support apple farmers in New York, its backing of various local and national cider making boards, as well as its creating educational opportunities, such as taking smaller, competing New York cider makers on trips to Europe to meet with traditional producers.

Perhaps Burk's biggest contribution to cider culture has been recognizing that cider makers may soon face a serious shortage of cider apples. Will there be enough bittersweet, bittersharp, and heirloom apples planted to satisfy the future demand of heritage cider? This worry is backed up by a 2018 report on the industry from Cornell University, warning that "the continued growth of the hard cider beverage market may be hampered by the lack of supply of specialized apples."

"Once you start making drier ciders, you need bittersweet apples," Burk told me. "Most cider makers don't have bittersweet apples. It's all about fruit and cultivation. People are trying to get this fruit into the ground and grow it." But that takes time. The best time to plant a tree was 20 years ago, goes the old Chinese proverb. The second-best time is now.

In response to the potential shortage, Angry Orchard funded a program in which it purchased 5,000 young cider apple trees from nurseries in the Finger Lakes and distributed them to smaller growers in that region. The company has also funded a Cornell University project, in partnership with the New York Farm Viability Institute, that studies the development of cider-specific orchards. The research will be made freely available to cider makers and orchardists across the country.

"It always disappoints me when people think we're this big Evil Empire," Burk said. "I'm deep in this community. I mean, we could *not* be planting hundreds of acres of bittersweet cider fruit."

Burk wanted me to taste some of his as-yet-unreleased experimental ciders, and so we walked into another red building full of barrels. Straight from the cask, we tasted a collaboration with Oliver's Cider, the cult producer from Herefordshire, England. This had been blended from four different vintages of bittersweet Dabinett apples and was aged in old Calvados barrels. It was big and funky, a cider with a figurative hairy chest and gold chain. Next, we tasted a sample made of 100 percent bittersweet Yarlington Mill apples. This had an amazing herbal, white pepper nose and was delicate on the palate. "I don't know what I'm going to do with this yet. But I think I want to bottle this all by itself," Burk said. From another cask, he drew a French-inspired cider called Dear Brittany, made from various Reinette bittersweets. "This I think is my favorite cider I've ever made," he said. Beautiful and balanced, it showed again that Burk is indeed a very good cider maker. At the same time, it was disquieting to see how disconnected these higher-quality ciders were from Angry Orchard's core business. Can you have it both ways?

On our way back to the Cider House, we walked through a chilly storage room full of apples. Burk grabbed a French variety called Amour Rouge and sliced it open, revealing surprising red flesh inside. "We're going to use this to make our rosé cider," he told me. Rosé wine has been a huge trend for half a decade, and Big Cider has been trying to follow the same playbook, pushing rosé cider as the drink of summer. Many of those early rosé ciders, however, got their pink coloring from additives. Now Angry Orchard was poised to jump on the rosé trend. But Burk said theirs would be different.

Sure enough, only a few months later, Angry Orchard Rosé Hard Cider launched. It wasn't as sweet as other Angry Orchard offerings, but it veered toward a tart, pink alcopop, with notes of watermelon Jolly Rancher, Sour Patch Kids, and strawberry lip gloss. It was certainly colored, in part, with red-fleshed apples. But if you looked at the list of ingredients on the label, it was also colored with sweet potato, radish, and hibiscus. Regardless, the Rosé Hard Cider was an immediate, massive hit. So successful, in fact, that its sales were cited by the corporate chairman on an investor call as a major factor in Boston Beer Company's strong turnaround in 2018.

* * *

Google Maps says that Angry Orchard's Innovation Cider House is only 22.7 miles from Aaron Burr Cidery. But that half-hour drive from Walden to Andy Brennan's house in the Catskills village of Wurtsboro may represent the widest philosophical chasm in the cider world. Angry Orchard may control 60 percent of the market, but Aaron Burr's in-demand, acclaimed bottles are some of the few ciders to appear on wine lists at luminary Michelin-starred restaurants like Eleven Madison Park, Gramercy Tavern, and Agern. The approaches could not be more different.

Brennan produces his micro-batch ciders almost solely with fruit that he forages from feral or abandoned trees in the Catskills and elsewhere. In fact, he and his wife, Polly Giragosian, only cultivate a relatively small number of young trees on their property, a historic farm that has Aaron Burr's name on the deed (he was the lawyer). Having one of America's most infamous historical figures on his cider labels is just the sort of cheeky gesture that Brennan loves to make. "My interest is in exploring what wild means. I'm anti-cultivation," he said. "Which means, of course, that I'm just one big hypocrite." I've spent a good deal of time with the 48-year-old Brennan—wandering the woods, picking fruit, and drinking cider with him—and he's alternately boyish and curmudgeonly, naive and intellectual, callow and wise. I still don't always totally know what to make of him.

"In the wild, trees are part of a natural location. It's the exact opposite of a farm where trees are forced to be somewhere," he said as we walked in the forested Mamakating Hollow, a few minutes from his home. "A tree independent of humans or human expectation is a better thing. Cider is just a way of proving that wild apples are better."

Our hike was part of a scouting excursion in early September, when Brennan decides which wild trees he will harvest. Mamakating Hollow is a historic but forgotten place. Washington Irving set one of his spooky ghost stories here in the 1830s, after visiting the area with vice president Martin Van Buren. "It's rumored that Johnny Appleseed crossed here in 1792, on his way from Massachusetts to Pennsylvania," Brennan said. "Now are these wild trees from seeds that he planted? We don't know. It's sort of like saying, 'George Washington slept here.'"

Brennan often talks about Johnny Appleseed (né John Chapman). "I consider myself a kindred spirit to Johnny Appleseed," he told me on several occasions. "I'm serving the tree. Forget the apples. Forget the cider. I just like being with trees." With his long, unkempt hair, graying beard, and droopy overalls, it often feels like he's channeling John Chapman, who railed against orchardists grafting apple trees. In *The Botany of Desire*, Michael Pollan quotes Chapman as once saying, "They can improve the apple in that way, but that is only a device of man, and it is wicked to cut up trees that way."

Brennan is more inscrutable. Just when you're about to latch onto the story of a modern-day John Appleseed, he'll reference his former life in New York, where he spent almost two decades as an artist, with a day job as an architect. "Commercial orchards are based on scale and certainty. I can't operate with that kind of certainty," he once told me. "Even when I paint, I paint with uncertainty. Think about Cézanne. Cézanne is uncertain, and he always keeps it open. That's what people hate about him. I want to be more like Cézanne, but of course I'm a weakling." It's no coincidence that Cézanne's most famous still lifes are of apples, and that he once said: "With an apple, I will astonish Paris."

We hiked along the old stone walls of what was once the Delaware & Hudson Canal, which was an engineering marvel when it opened in 1828, but ceased operation by the end of the 19th century, eclipsed by railroad travel. All along the canal footpath are the remnants of old farmsteads. Brennan wanted me to see a particular 160-year-old apple tree, one of his favorites. "It's dying a slow death, but I want you to see it." The footpath ended and suddenly the forest floor was choked with poison ivy. I am extremely allergic to poison ivy and break out badly at least once a year, so I was reluctant to tread through. Not Brennan. He clomped straight into the thickest patch, saying, "Poison ivy is just part of it. If harvesting these apples means I get a terrible poison ivy rash, well, that's just part of the experience. I feel like the fruit from this place needs to be represented in my ciders." Brennan also says that he gets *E. coli* about once a year from tasting apples that have fallen to the ground—also part of the experience.

He cleared some overgrowth and pointed out the foundation of an old farmstead. Just beyond stood the big old tree, looking in pretty bad shape. "Yep, it's dead," he said, forlornly. "It's totally dead." We did, however, locate several other healthy trees in the area, full of fruit, including one that must have been 60 feet tall. "Look at this enormous tree!" Brennan shouted. He jumped up and grabbed two gnarled little apples. We bit into them, and the taste was tannic and chalky, with such searing acidity that I had to spit it out. "Wow," he said. "That's going to make great cider!"

Transfixed by how many apples hung from this particular tree, Brennan broke into a monologue: "An apple tree is supposed to look like a bird feeding station. And the fruit that drops to the ground is meant to be eaten by large mammals. Apples are not meant for humans; they're meant for the deer, the bear, the horse, and the cow. That's why wild apples are small, hard, highly tannic, and acidic. They're meant to sit on the ground long enough for animals to come eat them. Apples are smart creatures. They have twice the genetic diversity that humans have." This is all true (anthropomorphism aside). Not too long ago, scientists did a sequencing of the Golden Delicious genome and discovered it had approximately 57,000 genes—the human genome only has around 20,000. Apples therefore show what's called "extreme heterozygosity," meaning their offspring almost never resemble, or taste like, their parents.

Not that Brennan has formal training in forestry, botany, or agriculture. He began foraging more than 20 years ago, when he was in college in Maryland, and squatted with a friend on the land of an old plantation owned by a 90-year-old farmer. They fished, gathered mushrooms, and picked wild fruit from an abandoned orchard. "I was basically homeless," he said. When the old man died, his nephew inherited the property and bulldozed the orchard. "He said he didn't want squatters like us on the property anymore." After that, Brennan moved to New York and lived the downtown artist's life, crashing on couches and sleeping on studio floors. His work as an architect dried up during the financial crisis of 2007–2008, along with his savings. At that point, he and Giragosian fled the city, and moved to the homestead in Wurtsboro. Giragosian has a day job teaching art at the local community college.

From Mamakating Hollow, we headed toward the Neversink Highlands, where we began to feel some altitude. For wine growing, we know that elevation offers more concentrated sunlight, dramatic temperature shifts, and excellent drainage, and there's evidence that altitude may hold similar key benefits for growing cider apples. Brennan handed me a thick soil atlas that was sitting on the dashboard, and he pointed out the Shawangunk Ridge, created 400 million years ago, that's full of limestone, shale, and quartz soils. "This is one of the greatest apple regions in the Western Hemisphere. There are more uncultivated apples here in the Catskills than there are cultivated ones in the Hudson Valley," he said.

Along the way, we scoped out potential trees for harvest. A distinction between abandoned, wild, and feral trees felt crucially important to Brennan. Each time he pulled his truck over, he would say things like: "These trees are abandoned. This was definitely an orchard." Or: "These trees have to be wild. There's no way a human planted this." At one open field, an old man in a truck eyed us warily. "This guy's an asshole. He's always paranoid," Brennan said, adding that there were lots of old retired mafia guys living around here. A few miles down the road, we passed a jeep with blinkers. "There's the crazy mail lady." As we wound through the hilly roads, we passed vacation homes and bungalow colonies with signs in Hebrew, owned by Orthodox Jews who have historically summered here in what was once the Borscht Belt. "Our population doubles in the summer," Brennan said. We passed a property with giant sculptures of nude men stacked totem-pole-like, in front of an old church building, with a sign that read, Church of the Little Green Man.

At one point, on a quarry road near the Neversink River called Dump Road, Brennan suddenly spotted a new tree he'd never seen, and pulled his truck off onto the shoulder. "I don't have a parking brake in this," he said, as he jumped out, the truck slowly rolling along with me in it. In less than a minute, he jumped back in with a handful of little golden apples that tasted like limes.

Along the Neversink River, we turned onto a dirt road and entered private property, where a farmer allows Brennan to forage. He drove to a hidden corner of the farm, and pulled the truck under the shade of a dozen gigantic trees. "You should have seen this place before. It was a jungle," he said. "We cleared it out so you could see rows. So it was probably an orchard many years ago." Several of the trees, Brennan estimates, are more than 200 years old. These feral apples represented reclaimed heritage. Perhaps the trees had been abandoned long ago by a farmer who couldn't find a market for his cider apples anymore, or whose heirs had no interest in orcharding and moved on to the city. We grabbed a couple of big red apples from one of the largest trees. They were much bigger than typical wild fruit, almost the size of eating apples. When I bit into one, the sharpness stung my lips and coated my teeth. "Wow, that's a mean apple," Brennan said. I don't know the precise difference between a "mean" apple and an "angry" apple, but this one was a true bittersharp, very rare to find, especially so large. Brennan has named this Denniston Red, and he makes single-varietal cider from it.

Underneath the thick branches of these old Denniston Red trees blocking out the sun, my mouth still stinging from this strange apple, it felt like we had stepped back into an essay by Henry David Thoreau, called "Wild Apples," that I'd recently read. "Every wild-apple shrub excites our expectations thus, somewhat as every wild child. It is, perhaps, a prince in disguise," Thoreau wrote. This essay came late in Thoreau's life, during the Civil War, and was published in *The Atlantic* a few months after his death. In "Wild Apples," he wistfully pays homage to the fruit he'd grown up foraging in rural New England. "The era of the Wild Apple will soon be past," he declared. "I see nobody planting trees today in such out-of-the-way places, along the lonely roads and lanes, and at the bottom of dell in the wood."

I asked Brennan if he'd ever read Thoreau's essay. "Of course," he said. "It's one of my favorites."

On the drive back to his house, I asked Brennan another question: Did it ever worry him that Angry Orchard might some day send an army of foragers up into the Catskills to gather all the wild apples to make one of its new heritage ciders. He was silent for a moment, and I couldn't tell if it had ever occurred to him. "Well, first of all, that would suck." He was silent for another few moments, but soon enough he spoke: "You know, even if Angry Orchard did that, I don't think it would work for them. I've spent so much time visiting these trees all year long. People say, 'You can't psychoanalyze a tree.' Well, I beg to fucking differ. You have to bond with the tree. You can't just be a greedy apple hoarder. I'm ingratiating myself into a system that already exists. It's the opposite of Western agriculture." Then, to finish a rant worthy of Johnny Appleseed himself, he said: "Cider makers are putting themselves at the mercy of the existing industrial agricultural system. Apples are the most sprayed fruit crop in America. Look at those apples grown on the worst chemically treated land. It's like Chinese foot binding. It's torture to the tree."

* * *

All the romance of foraged fruit wouldn't mean very much, obviously, if the cider made from it ended up tasting mediocre. But Aaron Burr's distinctive ciders can often be transcendent, as long as you're open to some funk, unfiltered cloudiness, and sediment. Which I, and many others, are.

When I returned to visit Brennan later in the fall, on a cold overcast day, he was in the cidery surrounded by dozens of boxes and crates of fruit. With a refractometer, he checked the brix of a tiny green apple. "This is just a seedling from a tree we call Ethel," he said.

He handed me another sharp little yellow one the size of a cherry. "This is a Witchie. It's from Holly Witchie's farm, so that's what I call it." According to Brennan, it's a rare variety, a so-called Siberian crab apple (or Manchurian crab) that's native to Russia and Central Asia, not North America—from the species *Malus baccata*, not the more common *Malus domestica* that Johnny Appleseed spread. Brennan is not sure whether it was planted once upon a time as an ornamental tree, or whether it's a seedling from random animal droppings.

We grabbed a bottle of his Malus Baccata cider, made from several varieties like Witchie, and we headed inside the house. Next to the woodburning stove, he poured the cider into three Mason jars, and he, Giragosian, and I began tasting. This particular Malus Baccata had been bottled in 2015 and was unbelievably tannic and complex, almost similar in structure to a young Barolo wine. "I guarantee you that this is still going to be drinkable 20 years from now," he said. Malus Baccata is Aaron Burr's most expensive cider: a 500-mililiter bottle sells for about $200.

Though Brennan has made cider at home for years, Aaron Burr only received its farm winery license from New York State in 2013. By the following year, after a bunch of favorable press, his ciders blew up among the hipster, natural-wine crowd in Brooklyn and Manhattan. "I have mixed emotions about the price," he said with a sigh. "It wasn't our goal to be exclusive or high-end. I just wanted to create a new set of parameters for cider. Ten years ago, the highest priced cider in the country was $20."

Price typically grows out of scarcity, and there just isn't a whole lot of Aaron Burr cider to go around. Brennan makes about 30 barrels a year, about 1,500 gallons, which is what he can produce from fruit that he physically picks himself. Once upon a time, he had a full-time employee, but hated the dynamic. "I felt bad," he said. "But it was so freeing when I finally fired him." All Aaron Burr cider rests in the bottle for at least a year before release.

The next bottles that Brennan opened were his Homestead Locational Ciders, such as Mamakating Hollow, East Branch, Neversink Highlands, and Taconic. "I like using 'locational' on the label, because terroir is a pretentious term," he said. "Cider doesn't have the pretentiousness of wine. It doesn't have the douchey vocabulary. I stick to the facts. This is tannic. This is tart. This has a darker color. Those are just facts."

Regardless, the *locational* differences are clear and distinct. The cider from Neversink Highlands is soft and fruity, with a little whiff of the pasture, the East Branch is dense and tannic, with a bitter amaro-like note on the finish, while the Mamakating Hollow—made with the last apples from that 160-year-old tree—is full of deep autumnal and wild berry notes. Brennan calls Taconic "a lava lamp of medium-gold goddess" and it's got sharp acidity and a bright fruity finish. All of these retail from between $20 and $40.

Aaron Burr Ciders can sometimes be challenging. Like Brennan himself, they can be polarizing to drinkers, and cider people around the Northeast all seem to have an opinion. Leif Sundström, whose Hudson Valley ciders are also beloved by the same hipster sommeliers, gave him a backhanded compliment: "When his ciders are great, they're fucking great. But occasionally they're oxidized and not totally clean." Sundström echoes a common refrain, but I've heard the same thing said about many coveted natural wines, too—mostly trash-talking among rival producers.

I particularly love the Taconic Homestead Locational Cider, with its high quotient of tart, tannic crab apples, in the mix. Brennan and Giragosian gathered these apples, literally, from along the Taconic and Bronx River Parkways near White Plains. "We were stuck in traffic one day, and I could see there were apples growing in the clover leaf off the exit. So we just pulled over and started picking."

Sometimes, when Brennan tells me things like this, I wonder if Aaron Burr is really only about apples, and foraging, and cider making. Sometimes, I wonder if this is all actually part of some large, elaborate performance art piece. On a couple of occasions, I've asked him if this is the case. Brennan laughed at the idea. "Maybe? I don't know!"

As tasting moved into drinking, the topic of Angry Orchard came up again, as it often does among cider people. While Brennan appreciated some of the experimental ciders that Ryan Burk was doing, he remained dubious. "They're trying to bridge the gap between industrial ciders and farm ciders," he said. "I guess I'm an asshole, because I just don't think there's a middle ground. They're living in a different economy, a different world. But what do I know? I've never borrowed money. I've never taken capital investment. I don't know anything about running a business. I can't ask the apple trees to do something they can't do."

Not long after Aaron Burr ciders had become the darlings of sommeliers and beverage directors, investors came knocking. Brennan and Giragosian actually met with a private equity firm. "They were real Wall Street people who wanted to, you know, *take us to the next level*." he said. "They wanted me to stop picking apples and just be the front man. But I love picking the apples. I love apple exploring. When I shared my vision with them, they said, 'You are not a professional. You're a hobbyist.' I took that as a compliment."

We had almost finished the cider that was made from fruit picked along the Taconic Parkway, and so Brennan opened a bottle of Sea Apples, his cider made from wild, sea-salt-kissed apples picked along the beach on a remote Maine island.

"I hate the idea of selling out," he said. "When I was younger, the biggest insult you could say to an artist was, 'You're a professional.' But it's all different now." Brennan and I are roughly the same age, and things were indeed different when we both came of age as Gen Xers during the early 1990s. I agreed about this idea of selling out. I told him that deep down, I also still believed that selling out was one of the worst sins, one I'd committed several times and felt shame about. We both acknowledged, though, that we were just old, nostalgic fogies. The whole notion of "not selling out" was a quaint one from a bygone era—so long gone that it may as well have been the era of Thoreau, Johnny Appleseed, or Cézanne.

As the sun set, Brennan fed some wood into the stove. Bone-chilling fall weather had definitely begun to arrive. "I'm just reluctant to watch the cider industry explode," he said. "There's something environmental and cultural at stake."

CHAPTER 4
THE CIDER MILL & THE CIRCUS

The beauty of cider lies in its simplicity: You pick apples, you grind them up, you press them, then you ferment the juice; after the fermented juice rests for a while, you bottle it. So whether apples are harvested from an orchard or from the wild, if you want to make cider, at some point, the fruit ends up in a press. Slipping deeper into the fall, I returned to the Finger Lakes, where cider makers were both picking and pressing.

On a brilliantly sunny, but crisp, October morning, I visited the Redbyrd cidery in Burdett, a few miles from Seneca Lake, not far from Shatt's orchard—the entire cidery squeezed into the corner of a farmhouse garage, across the road from a red barn full of cows. Wooden crates full of dozens of apple varieties stood stacked along the wall, with more in the back of a pickup truck. Inside, Eric Shatt dumped apples from a crate onto a well-worn wooden conveyor belt—red, yellow, and green ones, some with rough, brownish russeting, in all sizes, from racquetballs to tennis balls. The machine rumbled loudly, and Shatt wore protective earmuffs over his knit cap. Over the machine's noise, Shatt shouted that these apples would be for his high-end cider, Cloudsplitter. "There's a lot of Porter's Perfection and Wickson Crab in here!" he shouted. "Also some Dabinett, Gold Rush, Baldwin, Newtown Pippin! And some Ashmead's Kernel, Stoke Red, and Brown Snout!"

Apples traveled up the conveyor belt to a grinder, which chopped them up into a slurry of ground fruit, peels, stems, and seeds that cider makers called pomace (different from pomace in winemaking, which is the end by-product after pressing). After the grinder filled, Shatt opened a latch and dropped the pomace onto a rack with a plastic liner, wrapped in cloth. With blue rubber gloves, Shatt spread it evenly, covered it with cloth, and set another rack on top. Then he dumped more apples onto the conveyor belt and started the process over. Once the stack of racks grew to a sufficient height, he lowered the heavy weight of the press. Juice flowed out, over the edges, into a tub below. "We're doing this in multiple pressings!" he shouted. "Then we'll have three tanks of Cloudsplitter! That's when the craft and artistry comes in!"

Part of that craft and artistry will be in how the juice undergoes fermentation—when yeast eats the fruit sugars and converts them into alcohol. In Shatt's case, he will add Champagne yeast to the juice; other cider makers will add other sorts of yeast, or allow fermentation to start with ambient, natural yeast. Some cider makers will ferment almost all of the sugars for a bone-dry cider, while others may stop fermentation while there is still a percentage of residual sugar. Another part of the craft and artistry will happen once fermentation is finished. How will the various batches, pressed and fermented throughout the season, be blended? Finally, once blended, in what vessel will the cider age: steel tanks, wooden barrels, or inside the bottles themselves? And for how long?

Shatt's small rack-and-cloth press is an antique that dates to the 1950s. "I found it in the junkyard of a company that makes orchard equipment!" he shouted. Even an antiquated press is a luxury for many small cider makers. Historically, many don't even own a press. In apple country, the tradition has always been to take your fruit to the local cider mill. New York State has the largest number of them in the nation.

That's why, on another morning, I found myself at Gansz Farms Cider Mill, near Lyons, about 20 minutes north of Seneca Lake. I'd accompanied a young cider maker, Adam Stahl of Star Cider, to Gansz on the day when his apples were to be pressed. "All they do at Gansz is press cider," he told me. "Their heart and soul is in it." Stahl, whose day job is in information technology, wore a camouflaged John Deere hat. I was dressed similarly, in a flannel shirt and a farm-logoed baseball cap.

Stahl introduced me to the Gansz brothers, 74-year-old Ed and 72-year-old Tom, whose grandfather started the business in 1913. Both Ed and Tom were dressed, like us, in flannel shirts and baseball caps—the big difference being that theirs looked as though they'd been worn as work clothes for several decades. Similarly, their large 45-inch cider press is the same one the family built in 1924. The whole operation is run by one red tractor in the corner, connected to a system of belts and pulleys. "That tractor's been sitting there for 70 years," Tom said. "This tractor makes the most money on the farm, and it doesn't turn a wheel. Guys come in here and say, 'For chrissakes, that's the same tractor you had when I came here as a kid with my dad.'"

The family's cider mill has been located on the outskirts of Lyons since 1939. "When my dad built this, there were six other cider mills in Lyons," Ed told me. "Everyone in town said, 'You'll never make any cider out there.' Well, we're still here and they're all gone."

We watched as Stahl's apples were loaded onto the conveyor belt, climbed up to the grinder, and then the pomace was dumped onto the racks. Gansz Farms' racks, about 25 square feet, are at least three times the size of Shatt's at Redbyrd. After the racks were covered in cloth and stacked high enough, a huge press was lowered, with 175 tons of pressure squeezing out the juice. "Now we use nylon cloth," Tom said. "We used to use burlap. Those were heavier than hell. And they broke." He recalled a time, years ago, when a fellow from the insurance company was inspecting the property, and the burlap burst. "He got apple all over his suit!"

Years ago, everyone who grew apples saved some for fermentation. "In the 1940s and 1950s, all farmers made hard cider," Ed said, adding that a lot of the homemade stuff was rough. "Some of that stuff, you could put it on your salad instead of vinaigrette." As late as the 1970s, the Gansz family would drive to nearby Geneva with a truckful of cider, which they'd pump into barrels in customers' basements. The cost was $5: $2.50 for the barrel and $2.50 to fill it. "But that generation died off," Ed said. "The next generation didn't know what cider was."

The shutdown of upstate New York's traditional cider mills has been profound. For years, the production of cider had been declining. During the mid-20th century, the Gansz family would press as much as 80,000 gallons of cider during a fall season. By the 2000s, Gansz's production had dropped to around 13,000 gallons per year.

Then, in 2004, there was a bad outbreak of *E. coli* in the news tied to unpasteurized, non-alcoholic sweet cider from a mill in the town of Peru, near Lake Champlain, with 300 people sickened. This wasn't the first time; there had been cases in other states where deaths from contaminated sweet cider had occurred. Soon after, the state legislature of New York passed a law making it mandatory to pasteurize all raw, sweet, non-alcoholic cider. Unfortunately, that meant cider mills had to purchase ultraviolet processing units, which cost between $15,000 and $30,000. That expense, and the liability, was the last straw for a lot of family cider mills, and many closed down.

But the Gansz family invested in the UV pasteurization equipment. A few years later, a new customer appeared on the scene: cider revivalists looking to make a craft beverage. Demand jumped, first to 23,000 gallons in 2015, then to more than 30,000 gallons in 2017. "I can't believe how much cider there is now," said Ryan Gansz, Ed's 33-year-old son. "The growth is all driven by craft cider makers and distillers. And it's a lot better and a lot easier pressing hard cider."

That's because juice to be used for alcoholic cider does not have to undergo pasteurization—UV or otherwise. *E. coli* and other bad bacteria won't survive alcoholic fermentation.

Ryan Gansz had originally been focused on the family farm's other crops, such as corn, soybeans, organic vegetables, and organic feed for livestock. But as the cider trend peaked, he joined his father and uncle in the mill. "It was either get interested or close up. Those guys aren't going to able to do this forever. This place was dying. They were messing around with a couple hundred gallons of cider." Ryan updated the equipment, adding plastic boards to the wooden racks and doubling the amount so they can run continuously, with little downtime. Now the mill averages more than 700 gallons per day from September through December, often doing as much as 900 gallons.

The new-wave craft cider makers do occasionally present a novel challenge for an 80-year-old cider mill. "They're fussy about their apples," Ed said. Some bring in crab and wild foraged apples of strange sizes and shapes, some of which are difficult to keep from falling through the machine. "One guy, he comes in here the other day and brings these tiny apples that look like frickin' cherries."

* * *

Since his fruit would be pressed for several more hours at Gansz Farms Cider Mill, Adam Stahl and I drove to his cidery, 20 minutes down the road, in Clifton Springs. Adam, 32, and his wife, Cortni Stahl, 29, started Star Cider in 2014. That same year, they sold their home to fund the start-up and moved into an Airstream trailer on his grandfather's farm. "My grandparents think we are absolutely nuts," Adam said. Their cidery is inside a converted garage, near where the Airstream sits in the yard.

I'd met Adam and Cortni on a visit to the Finger Lakes the winter before, when I was researching my wine book. At that time, I was impressed by how eager and enthusiastic they were about the cider revival. "This is so exciting to see cider happening in our own lifetime!" Adam said. "We're building the culture right now. It will be written in the history books that the Finger Lakes is where it began!"

As we tasted their Northern Spy and Golden Russet from the tank, they told me how they'd begun as home cider makers. "My tipping point was when Adam shattered five gallons of cider fermented with blackberries in the basement," Cortni said. "That's when I said, 'We have to do this for real, or stop.'"

Cortni's day job is in Cornell University's Enology Extension Lab in Geneva. She's worked for brewers and distillers and was head cider maker at Blue Toad Hard Cider. "He grows the trees; I make the booze," she said. When I visited Cortni at her lab, she told me that Cornell was researching apple tannins, how we perceive bitterness and astringency, how it can be measured in cider. "There are so many things we need to learn," she said. "Tannins are an important component of most high-end ciders. But we don't even know how to measure it, correlated with sensory analysis and perception."

At his grandparents' farm, Adam gave me a tour of the Airstream, as well as the small orchard he'd begun planting. Right next to the Airstream were about 100 young trees—Roxbury Russet, Cox's Orange Pippin, Stembridge Jersey, and Kingston Black among them. "This is the second year they've been in the ground," he said. "This is for us to study and learn."

Adam and Cortni had gone to Eric Shatt at Redbyrd for help. "There's no published guidance," Adam said. "So we brought Eric an apple pie and sought some wisdom." Shatt gave them scion wood from his trees so the Stahls could start their own orchards—including his domesticated wild apple, Gnarled Chapman. "The cider industry in the Finger Lakes is so supportive." As they wait for their own trees to bear fruit, Star Cider has been sourcing apples from various local orchards in the region, and selling a mix of heritage and modern ciders in kegs, mostly available in nearby towns. In this way, Adam and Cortni Stahl are illustrative of a new generation of cider makers.

Within the United States Association of Cider Makers, more than a quarter of its members classify themselves as "cidery-in-planning"—meaning these are amateurs with dreams of turning pro. These cideries-in-planning are likely similar to the Stahls before they got licensed and began selling to the public. The sheer number of cideries-in-planning suggests that the era of craft cider has only just begun. In New York State alone, there are about 90 licensed cideries, more than any other state in the nation. That number has more than doubled since 2014.

During Finger Lakes Cider Week, I'd attended a public event where Adam and Cortni were pouring their ciders at a place called Water Side Wine Bar in the nearby town of Phelps. Besides Star Cider, there were others present: Lake Drum Brewing (established in 2015); Blue Toad Hard Cider (established in 2015); and Embark Craft Ciderworks (established in 2015). Mostly, these cideries focus on modern cider, sold in cans and kegs. Blue Toad, which makes cider in both New York and Virginia, served its ROC HARD Amber and Flower City Blonde, as well as ones flavored with blueberry and black cherry. Embark comes from a family farm in Williamson (the hometown of Angry Orchard's Ryan Burk) and the brand's sales rep served the cidery's American Hopped Cider and Blueberry Peach Cider. The cider makers of Lake Drum, from nearby Geneva, sampled sumac- and currant-flavored ciders, alongside their single-varietal Northern Spy.

Adam and Cortni poured their Apple Crisp, flavored with a blend of spices "borrowed from our Grandmother's apple crisp recipe." They'd been having decent local success with Apple Crisp, and I saw it on tap at some bars in Geneva and Ithaca. They also poured their ginger-flavored cider, as well as one called Frisky Whiskey, which had aged one year in a whiskey barrel. For this consumer event, however, they did not pour their dry Appley Ever After, a blend of foraged wild crabs and Golden Russet that goes through a Champagne-style second fermentation in the bottle.

"One of my life goals is to get people to drink less commercial," Adam had told me when we were at Gansz Farms Cider Mill. This evangelical mission would have to wait for another day. On that afternoon at the Water Side Wine Bar, the crowd was sparse—only four people showed up during the first hour or so. But closer to happy hour, more people arrived. I heard a few people ask Cortni, "What's your sweetest cider?"

* * *

"Fall seems like the only time of year to get people interested in cider," said Melissa Madden, co-owner of the Finger Lakes Cider House and its label Kite & String. "It's so hard to reach new consumers outside the fall season." Madden bemoaned this reality, since the fall season of an orchardist and cider maker is filled with the essential work of harvesting and pressing apples. For Madden, there are also promotional appearances at cider festivals, hand-selling at farmers markets, and running a U-Pick orchard on weekends—not to mention several hundred visitors to her tasting room and restaurant on weekends. "It's crazy and it can be a pain in the ass. It's our busiest work season and we also have to be promoting because it's the only time of year that people are thinking about apples." That consumer mentality is an odd phenomenon for cider. Consider that grapes are also harvested in the fall. Yet no one would think that the only time to drink cabernet sauvignon or pinot grigio is during a window from September through December. Certain popular wines like prosecco or rosé don't even enter the conversation until the weather turns warm. Yet cider remains rooted in the autumn of the popular imagination, pigeonholed with pumpkin patches, bobbing for apples, and mulled grog.

Madden and I were having dinner on a cold, quiet Monday, along with her business partner—and ex-husband—Garrett Miller, at a restaurant called Hazelnut Kitchen, in Trumansburg. Quirky and quaint, Trumansburg might be my platonic ideal of a village: several decent bars, a bookstore, a bowling alley, a great coffee shop, a Wednesday evening farmers market, a bus to the university town of Ithaca, and close proximity to dozens of wineries, cideries, and distillers.

Hazelnut Kitchen is a wonderfully low-key, farm-to-table spot with a great list of local wines and ciders. The staff had paired four Kite & String ciders with our meal, beginning with an off-dry bottling from 100 percent Baldwin apples that was perfect with a spicy, creamy pepper soup. That was followed by rabbit confit with acorn and butternut squash, paired with Cazenovia, a bone-dry blend of Dabinett, Northern Spy, Chisel Jersey, and a variety of crab apple called Pioneer. Cazenovia (named after a fertile soil of the region) is a serious, complex, structured sparkling cider with razor-sharp acidity made in the traditional Champagne method. Finally, there was a pork shoulder with herb spätzle paired with bone-dry Geneva Russet, also made *methode champenoise*, but rounder, creamier, honeyed, more like a chardonnay-based Blanc des Blancs. A meal like that highlighted what an underrated pairing cider can be—almost always better than beer, and often better than wine.

What I love about Kite & String's ciders is their attractive acidity and wine-like levels of alcohol by volume. They, like many in the

Finger Lakes, produce ciders with alcohol by volume nearing nine or 10 percent. This isn't just boozy talk: Alcohol is sort of like fat or salt in cooking; it makes flavors pop. But it has to be in balance. In fact, I generally dislike many bruising, high-alcohol wines that come from hotter climates—mainly because they don't pair well with food. Cider has the opposite problem. Since it's been sold as a beer alternative for so long, the alcohol level in most ciders hovers, gulpably, around five or six percent. That doesn't really work at the table as a food pairing, especially alongside rich fall dishes. Miller said he believes that, as growing practices evolve, cider apples in the Finger Lakes can someday produce ciders with the same alcohol level as the local white wines. Yet this power comes with a price. Any cider over 8.5 percent alcohol is subject to federal excise taxes. "We just paid a really, really big tax bill," Madden said.

The day after our dinner at Hazelnut, I visited Madden in her more natural environment, her organic farm, which surrounds Finger Lakes Cider House. Madden is short and wiry, with ripped, muscular arms and blonde hair usually pulled into a tight braid. She resembles the ideal of a horsewoman, which makes sense since she likes to farm with draft horses. In fact, at the start, she only farmed with horses, planting all 4,000 of their apple trees with them. But at a certain point, in 2015, Madden and Miller broke down and bought a tractor.

As many young people who've ventured into the cider business quickly learn, the path is not an easy one—especially for those who don't own family orchards. Madden and Miller bought their property, Good Life Farm, in 2008. At the time they were married, and for six years, the couple lived off the grid, with no electricity. Most of the apple trees they planted took a half decade to become established, a few even longer. "Some of the trees that we planted ten years ago, we're still waiting to get fruit," Madden said. But the learning curve for the cider business was steep. Originally, their cider brand was also called Good Life, until they found themselves in a trademark dispute with a larger company. So they had to rename the brand and design new labels. When they opened Finger Lakes Cider House in 2015, it operated sort of like a co-op, offering from various local producers, such as Eve's, South Hill, Black Diamond, and Redbyrd. But the logistics of that model proved challenging. Now, the tasting room mostly pours Kite & String, with a regular rotation of guest ciders. Meanwhile, Good Life Farm maintains a mix of organic agriculture, raising turkeys and beef cattle, growing ginger and other crops, including all the vegetables and herbs for the Cider House's kitchen. "It's exhausting," Madden said. "Sometimes it's too much." Despite the hurdles and setbacks, Kite & String is now represented by Skurnik Wines, one of the nation's powerhouse importers and distributors.

After the farm tour, Madden led me downstairs, underneath the Cider House tasting room, to the cidery. Miller and his brother Jimmy were there disgorging the lees, or dead yeast particles, out of the Funkhouse, an important step for Champagne-method bottlings. Before the second fermentation in bottle, Funkhouse is made with a third of the cider aged in charred American oak barrels. As he gripped the bottles and casually popped open one after another, in his short sleeves, muscles and tattoos on display, Miller exuded the physicality and aloofness of a quarterback taking snaps in practice.

Madden seemed surprised by the disgorging. "And why are we doing this today?" she asked, tersely.

"Well," said Miller, as he popped open another bottle. "We're out of Funkhouse."

Madden and I went upstairs to taste through more of the Kite & String portfolio, including a good single-varietal bottling of Northern Spy, and a fantastic still cider called Glacial Till, riesling-like and full of zest and minerality. I was also excited to try Pioneer Pippin, which had recently won New York's first Governor's Cup for cider. This is a blend of heirloom Newtown Pippin and high-acid, high-tannin crab apples, including Manchurian crabs (i.e., *Malus baccata*)—"a glimpse into that crazy, exponentially expanding world of apple genetics we continue to geek out about," wrote Madden in her cider club newsletter. Even though Pioneer Pippin is semi-dry, with a bit of residual sugar, it's a thrilling cider, full of unique contrast and tension.

Beyond taste, it was fascinating to see Kite & String using Newtown Pippin in so many blends. This old variety was discovered as a seedling (or "pippin") in the late 17th or early 18th century in what is now the New York City borough of Queens. In early America, Newtown Pippin was widely grown and praised. George Washington grew them, and Ben Franklin took barrels of them with him to London, prior to the Revolution. When Thomas Jefferson was in Paris, he wrote, "They have no apples here to compare with our Newtown Pippin." Queen Victoria loved Newtown Pippins so much that, in 1838, she lifted the tariff on imported American apples. Eventually, Newtown Pippin fell out of favor as a green eating apple, overtaken by the Granny Smith, which originated in Australia in 1868, and exploded in popularity in the US in the 1980s. Yet, oddly enough, Newtown Pippin is still grown in significant quantities, mostly because it's one of the main apples used in Martinelli's sweet sparkling cider. In fact, when Martinelli's first started, in the 1860s, the company made real cider—before pivoting to sweet during Prohibition.

Not long after that visit to the Finger Lakes Cider House, I returned and had a drink separately with Miller. As Madden was plowing a field with her horses, Miller and I sat on the deck and, though he is a man of few words, we chatted about apples and cider making. At one point, he disappeared downstairs, then returned with an unlabeled bottle. He told me it was "an experiment" and to let it rest a few days before opening. When I popped open the bottle a few nights later and tasted it, the cider was like nothing I had tried before. It had a crazy, complex, almost tropical nose, stinging acidity, and a unique briny element on the palate. The strange experience was like that of drinking Muscadet wine from the Loire, which happens to be a classic pairing with oysters.

I texted Miller my tasting notes. I wanted to know what this mystery cider was. "It's a single variety dessert apple called Gold Rush," he texted back. Gold Rush is, in fact, a modern dessert apple, created in 1972 in a lab at Purdue University from a cross between the ubiquitous Golden Delicious and another unnamed apple. It's not an heirloom, not a bittersweet, not a bittersharp. Therefore, as a cider variety, Gold Rush contradicts all the common cider-making wisdom.

Miller insisted that simply relegating Gold Rush to "dessert apple" status was a mistake. "'Dessert' doesn't really do it justice," he texted. He insisted that even some so-called dessert apples could be useful cider apples—if they are grown in excellent terroir, such as that in the Finger Lakes. "With apples," he insisted, "I think we really haven't scratched the surface on the effect of agricultural practices on flavor."

* * *

Blackduck Cidery sits only eight minutes up the road from the crowds at Finger Lakes Cider House—but it is miles apart in philosophy. A hand-painted sign declares, in all caps, *NO BUS NO LIMO.* "We make all the things you're not supposed to," said John Reynolds, Blackduck's cider maker. "I'm the black sheep of the Finger Lakes. I'm an anarchist." He certainly inhabits the role, with a thick beard falling somewhere between Friedrich Engels and a young Fidel Castro, a poster of Spain's anarchist Confederación Nacional del Trabajo party hanging in the tasting room, and a cider labeled *¡No Pasarán!*—the revolutionary slogan used during the Spanish Civil War and Sandinista-era Nicaragua.

Most of the best cider makers in the Finger Lakes, and elsewhere, are organic, but Reynolds takes it a step further, relying solely on wild fermentation, with no added yeast, and minimal sulfites. His ciders are often cloudy, with sediment at the bottom. "I hate Champagne-method cider," he said. In this way, Reynolds is the cider equivalent of the fervent natural winemakers that stir the hearts of hipster wine lovers in big cities. His range of ciders is certainly anarchic, from acidic, Spanish-style *¡No Pasarán!* to a funky English-style cider called Percy Percy to some ciders that aren't even made from apples at all. While most producers use a small, judicious percentage of super tart, sharply tannic crab apples, Reynolds offers one cider, Crabby Pip, in which crab apples make up nearly half the blend, decidedly a cider for so-called acid hounds. When I visited during pressing, Reynolds had me taste from a tank of 100 percent crab apples. The acid and tannins nearly ripped my mouth off. "I could drink this all day," he said. "I thought about bottling this as is. But everyone would hate it. Even the hipsters in Brooklyn."

I've spent a good deal of time with 47-year-old Reynolds, and I've come to realize that there's usually some calculation to the anarchy. For instance, the crab apple harvests over the past few years in the Finger Lakes has been excellent. "I see crab apples as being a more consistent source of tannins here in America," he told me. "They're more resistant to fungal diseases and fire blight, and they're less likely to go biennial."

Fire blight and biennialism are two huge problems for orchardists. Fire blight is a contagious bacterial disease that infects apple and pear trees, at first causing the leaves and blossoms to shrivel and turn black, then spreads throughout the limbs and trunk, eventually killing the tree. Biennialism, or biennial bearing, is when apple and pear trees simply stop producing fruit in certain years, creating irregular crop harvests. This could be due to growing conditions like drought or low-nutrient soil or possibly due to the tree simply bearing too much fruit one year and exhausting itself. The idea that indigenous crab apples might have more of a resistance to fire blight or biennialism is a fascinating, though unproved, hypothesis.

On this unseasonably warm late-fall day, Reynolds was grinding Kingston Black apples to be pressed. These were apples he'd been "sweating" for 10 days. Sweating, which many producers do, is to let the fruit sit in a warm, dry place so it desiccates and sheds some water. When apples sweat, sugars develop further, and the aromatics heighten. But if the fruit sits too long, bad microbial things can happen. "It's a big decision, to let the apples sit for days or weeks," he said.

Normally, after grinding, the pomace would be pressed right away, separating the juice from the skins, stems, and seeds—similar to making white wine. But Reynolds does things a little differently, allowing the chopped-up apple to macerate for several days before pressing. This is how Spanish cider is made, in Asturias and the Basque region. "This is quite different from what most cider makers do," Reynolds said. "People are always like, 'that's scary.' But it's not scary. It's how red wine is made. I'm just trying to mimic the Asturian style in my own simple way." When it's time to press, instead of a rack-and-cloth machine, Reynolds uses what's called a bladder press: a stainless steel cylinder with lots of tiny holes; once ground, the pomace is stuffed inside and then a bladder is inflated, pressing the pomace against the cylinder walls until juice runs out.

It was a weekday, and Reynolds' two homeschooled daughters ran barefoot around the farm. Both redheads, the oldest one is

Idunn, named after the Norse goddess who keeps the golden apples, and the little one is named Pippin. At first, they played on a big pile of mulch in the parking lot, but then Idunn locked Pippin in the Porta Potty. Pippin started crying. "Don't lock your sister in the Porta Potty!" Reynolds scolded.

"Papa, do you have any apples I can eat?" asked Idunn. "Me too!" shouted Pippin, dashing free of the Porta Potty. He handed each of them a yellowish-brown Ashmead's Kernel. Soon after, Reynolds' wife, Shannon O'Connor, arrived to pick up the girls. O'Connor is the director of the local library in Ovid, as well as manager of the cidery business. "I'm the reason he can make cider," she said. "Yeah," he said. "She's the one with a job." Like most other cider makers in the Finger Lakes, they're relatively new, first bottling and selling to the public in 2013.

Reynolds was working as a plant breeding specialist in Cornell's horticulture department when he planted his first fruit trees 18 years ago. Now, he and O'Connor have three parcels, including a home farm with 14 acres of mostly apples and pears, but also cherries, berries, plums, as well as some more exotic fruit. They manage two other orchards, both with over 100-year-old trees. "I'm a fruit grower first, and cider maker second," he said.

In fact, Reynolds' first love is perry, or pear cider, and that's where he often begins his tasting, with his hazy, unfiltered Wild Perry, showing a surprising balance of piercing acidity and creaminess, with green notes of celery and sage, along with serious tannins. "For me, perry is always a more complex drink than apple cider," he said.

But Reynolds doesn't stop at pears. Over the course of a tasting, he will pour crazy, often-transcendent co-fermentations made from blending apple with fruits such as local riesling grapes or sea buckthorn or ground cherries. He makes a cider called Black Flag with black currants and one called Red Flag with red currants. Then there's Aronious, his cider made with a bit of aronia, or chokeberry, juice—a strange, savory cider with black olive and dill notes, like a cabernet franc wine. He just started blending quince from trees he planted several years ago. "And medlar fruit is definitely something I'm tempted to plant."

Nothing divides the cider community more than the idea of non-apple bottlings. "Some people see adding anything besides apples as blasphemy. Then there's wild experimentation. I guess I see myself as somewhere in the middle," Reynolds said. "The sky's the limit. But the question always will be, 'When is it not cider anymore?'"

Blackduck is just one of many cideries experimenting with other fruits. Perry in particular has a long tradition in the English counties of Herefordshire, Gloucestershire, and Worcestershire, and its French cousin *poiré* has historically been produced in Normandy alongside cider and Calvados. Brands like Oliver's Classic Perry from Herefordshire and Christian Drouin Poiré from Normandy are mainstays on cider lists around the country. Even Eve's Cidery has made pear cider for years. In fact, I tasted one with Autumn Stoscheck made with 50 percent foraged wild pears, from a tank labeled "Skelepear." When I wondered what that name was all about, Autumn told me that her son, Zuri, had recently told her that she needed cooler labels. So she suggested that he name this one. Since Zuri loves skeletons, it was decided that Skelepear would be the name.

Pears, along with apples, can still be legally labeled as cider. Everything else must be labeled as fruit wine. But there's plenty that one can add to an apple or pear cider base. I once did a tasting with Adam and Cortni Stahl at a brewpub called Lake Drum Brewing, in Geneva, at the tip of Seneca Lake. The Stahls poured me delightful apple ciders flavored with juice from sour cherries, strawberries, rhubarb, and even a hibiscus-ginger cider, made with organic ginger grown at Good Life Farm. Lake Drum makes good cider alongside its beers, and the co-owner, Victor Pultinas, poured his Undercurrant, an apple cider fermented with black currants, and a wonderful cider spiced with sumac. "Cider is so malleable. That's why it's so great," Pultinas said.

"In some cider circles, we're an abomination," Adam said. "People say, 'Why would you take a perfectly good cider and add fruit?' But the consumer is demanding variety." However, he added: "You have to use fruit that's real."

Even Dan Pucci, pommelier at the hallowed Wassail, had more than 20 non-apple ciders on his menu. He insisted on keeping an open mind, but added, "I don't carry things that are flavored for the sake of flavor, or are synthetically flavored. We won't have a mango-habanero cider."

What's disturbed many cider people is that Big Cider has leaped headlong into the flavored cider trend. Within the craft cider community, there is the perception that some producers add artificial flavorings and additives—what many in the industry call "adjuncts"—to cheap, bulk juice concentrate. Large producers insist that the consumer wants more choices. "Straight-up apple ciders can be one-dimensional in taste. People can get tired of them. They want more flavors—a wider variety of fruits," is what Jeffrey House, owner of California Cider Company, told the drinks trade magazine *Market Watch* a few years ago. House's brand, Ace, makes ciders flavored with pineapple, honey, and pumpkin, among others. It's a curious admission for Big Cider to make, that cider made from sweet dessert fruit is "one-dimensional." Yet instead of seeking out better apples, or taking more care in the cider making, some companies' "solution" is to roll out gimmicky flavors.

Purists like Melissa Madden at Kite & String take a dim view. "Some people use the other fruits to mask low-quality cider," she said. "It's a trend none of us want to get involved with. It's become a circus. It's frustrating." Having said that, Madden sheepishly poured a glass of Nor'easter, her own cider that's flavored with cranberries. "This is where we go down a slippery slope," she said, with a chuckle. "But we do have a friend on Cape Cod who has a cranberry bog. And we home juice the cranberries. I guess the question for us is: Who's growing the fruit?"

Andy Brennan at Aaron Burr Cidery, unsurprisingly, took a similar position. "Flavoring ciders or creating these 'recipe ciders' is similar to beer making, where it becomes about the prowess of the brewer, or the cider maker," Brennan said, adding that he "hated the ease with which cider can be manipulated." Still, even Brennan makes a cider called Appinette, which is a blend of apples and traminette wine grapes. And for few years, one of his bestselling bottles was a ginger-carrot-apple cider. When I asked about the ginger-carrot-apple, he sighed and said, "I stopped making that two years ago out of concern for how cider was portrayed. Admittedly, that's a dumb reason."

A few years ago, I wrote an article about non-apple ciders for the *New York Times*, and I quoted both Brennan and Madden as naysayers to non-apple ciders. In response, Reynolds—clearly relishing his role as a troublemaker—created two ciders named for the dissenting purists. The first cider, for Brennan at Aaron Burr, was made with apples and gewürztraminer grapes; he labeled that Hamilton's Revenge. The second cider, for Madden, was a bit stranger, a riff on her disparaging quote, *It's become a circus*. In that, he fermented a small amount of ground cherries, a tiny fruit with a husk like a tomatillo that tastes sweet and tropical, somewhere between a pineapple and a cherry tomato. The name for this strange cider: Circus.

* * *

Though the beauty of cider may lie in its simplicity, later that fall I had a chance to see just how complicated cider can become. I found myself in a conference room of the lakefront Ramada Plaza in Geneva, observing Cornell University's Cider & Perry Production "master class," taught by Peter Mitchell. Mitchell has worked in the cider industry for 30 years, both in the UK and here in the US, and his client list includes Bulmers, Heineken, Diageo, and Angry Orchard. His five-day course costs $2,000, plus travel and accommodations, and people from all over the country attend. I'd been invited to sit in by Cortni Stahl from Star Cider, since her employer, the Enology Extension Lab, administers the course.

On the afternoon I observed, about two dozen students had broken into several small groups for a simulated product development trial. Each group was given a pitcher of what they called "base cider." Cortni's boss at the lab, Chris Gerling, told me, "They're all given a basic fermented cider and they'll make something exotic. Well, it doesn't have to be exotic. Each group identified a market segment. They're working on a concept and a consumer trial. Then they will calculate materials and costs to scale."

Privately, Cortni told me that the "base cider" was actually hers. "It's probably what we pressed that day at Gansz Farms when you were there with Adam," she said.

Once the base cider was passed around, Peter Mitchell addressed the group. "Don't be afraid of water. Adding water increases drinkability," Mitchell said. "You will be able to carbonate. When you blend the carbonation you want to blend it when it's lacking acidity. Carbonation puts more body into cider." He motioned toward a table full of ingredients—alongside the water and the carbonation device sat apple juice concentrate, molasses, honey, demerara and turbinado sugars, agave nectar, ReaLemon ("100% lemon juice"), and fructose. "You've also got citric and malic acid. And you have some tartaric acid." Then, before he set the groups loose, he offered a caution of sorts: "You've got a good base. A very good base to start with. If you can't do something with this base . . . I don't know. . . ."

As the groups got to work, I overheard someone at a table exclaim, "I like this idea! It's like the Corona of cider!" Another group was targeting "wine crossovers." Mitchell suggested to them, "Think pinot grigio." I ended up following a group whose target market was "millennials."

"It might make sense to bring the alcohol by volume down to around five percent," said a guy named Alec Steinmetz who worked at Graft cidery in Newburgh, New York.

"Yeah, something more sessionable," said a guy named Kyle Degener, from near Lexington, Kentucky, who'd just planted an orchard close to Maker's Mark Distillery, and would soon start a cidery.

"It just doesn't seem very craft to add water," said Steinmetz. "But we do need to bring down the ABV?"

"Wait, why are we bringing down the ABV?" asked Brandon Cline, a Southern Californian who now lives in Nashville, where he's planning to open a cidery.

"Well, there's the idea that millennials want something social and easy drinking," Degener said.

The base cider was just over seven percent alcohol by volume, and so the group decided to add apple juice concentrate and agave nectar. They tasted. "That's a little harsh," Cline said.

"Yeah," Degener said. "This would definitely benefit from some carbonation."

"OK," Steinmetz said. "But I don't think acid is the answer."

They added fifteen more drops of agave nectar. "The kids like it sweet," Degener said.

All agreed that the addition of the agave syrup was a good idea. "I don't know if it's tricking me," Degener said. "But this definitely is more pleasurable."

"But do you think we should add anything more?" Cline asked. "Simpler might be better."

"I say we stay with the 15 drops of agave, and then double the concentrate," Steinmetz said. They added more concentrate and tasted.

"Mmmm. Pretty good," Degener said. "Not my cup of tea, but it's good."

Suddenly something occurred to Cline. "Hmmm," he said. "Do you think millennials are going to want apple juice concentrate in their cider?"

I didn't stay through the entire product development trial. To be honest, it got a little boring when the groups had to calculate all the materials and costs to scale. Throughout the fall, I described what I'd observed to a few cider makers, including Autumn Stos-check and John Reynolds. "Peter Mitchell is so hugely influential," said Autumn. "But with that approach, the raw material could be anything. It could just be malt liquor."

Reynolds was even more dismissive. "I can always taste when a cider maker has gone to Peter Mitchell's class," he said. "The approach feels like a cookbook recipe. I would find no joy in that."

* * *

After spending some time in Mitchell's class with aspiring cider makers from other parts of the country, I realized that I needed to fan out from New York. I wanted to see what was going on in New England, the Pacific Northwest, Michigan, Virginia, and elsewhere. I also knew I needed to make pilgrimages to the traditional cider cultures in places like Spain and France. Sad as I was to leave the Finger Lakes, I knew it was time for my cider journey to continue further.

On my way home, I stopped one more time in the village of Trumansburg, for coffee. I backed into the parking spot too quickly, and my tire hit the curb roughly. By the time I came out of the coffee shop, I had a completely flat tire. At precisely the moment that I realized the tire was flat, a pickup truck full of apple crates pulled up behind me. Steve Selin, the cider maker of South Hill, whom I'd previously been foraging with, jumped out, buzzing with excitement. "I found this great new place to pick!" he said. "This accountant called me up about these apple trees he planted in his yard 20 years ago. Look! The guy's got Golden Russets, Roxbury Russets, Rhode Island Greening, Esopus Spitzenburg, Calville Blanc, and all kinds of unidentifiables! Beautiful apples!"

Suddenly, Selin looked down. "Oh man, your tire's flat." Without a second's thought, he opened my trunk, and fished around for the jack and the spare. "Here, I'm already all dirty anyway, I'll help you fix your tire." Within fifteen minutes, Selin had me on my way. I was a little embarrassed—I am capable of fixing a tire—but the gesture was so amazingly kind. It was the sort of thing I'd been encountering over and over with cider people. After years of covering wine and high-end spirits, it was often shocking how downright *nice* cider people are.

As he fixed my flat, I told Selin about my visit to Gansz Farms Cider Mill, and how Ed Gansz had been complaining about a guy who brought him apples that "looked like frickin' cherries." Selin laughed out loud. "Those were my apples," he said.

CHAPTER 5
PIPPIN AIN'T EASY

I'm not exactly sure why I picked up a copy of the *Old Farmer's Almanac*, with its gee-whiz trivia and corny humor, on my way to the 24th annual Franklin County Cider Days. But surely, as I drove through Western Massachusetts on my way, past white churches with pointy steeples, clapboard homes, red barns, and trees emblazoned with hues of golds and oranges, I must have been moved by some archetypal vision of New England, like something out of *Yankee Magazine*, which happens to be a sponsor of Cider Days and the publisher of the *Old Farmer's Almanac*.

I didn't crack it open until Sunday morning, when I sat in my hotel room in Greenfield, Massachusetts, not far from the Vermont border, slightly hungover from consuming so much of Cider Days' offerings. The *Old Farmer's Almanac* is the oldest continuously published periodical in North America, founded in 1792 during the George Washington administration. What's immediately striking about the *Almanac* is that the cover has not changed much since a redesign that happened in 1851. Since then, the book has remained yellow, with the title still flanked by the solemn drawings of Benjamin Franklin and the *Almanac's* founder Robert B. Thomas. The four corners are adorned with old-fashioned renderings of the four seasons, beginning clockwise from the left with spring. About the only thing missing from the *Almanac* these days is the old hole that used to be punched straight through the upper left-hand corner of every copy, so it could hang on a farmhouse hook. Even the guides to weather, frost, and growing seasons, tides, best fishing days, and arti-cles such as "The ABCs of Pickling," "The Pros and Cons of Backyard Livestock," "How to Make Sausage at Home," and "How Well Do You Know the Mockingbird?" could easily have turned up in a mid-19th century edition. There was even a game where you had to identify apple varieties hidden in a short story called "An Apple Romance." (I found four in the first two sentences: "The *duchess* and *Ben Davis* went on a date. They met at the *Blue Pearmain*, a tea room on the bank of the *Wolf River*.")

As I consulted the "calendar of the heavens"—the predictive heart of the *Almanac*—I learned that yesterday had been Sadie Haw-kins Day. Had I not been drinking cider, the *Almanac* advised that it would have been a good day to undergo dental care, to quit smoking, and to wean animals or children. Looking forward to Tuesday, the day of the midterm elections, it would be a favorable day to breed animals, to slaughter livestock, and to can, pickle, or make sauer-kraut. The following Monday would be an agreeable day to begin logging, to set posts, or to pour concrete. Ten days from then would be optimal for castrating animals.

I had no reason to believe otherwise. Sunday was daylight sav-ing time, and the sun had risen at 6:21 A.M., precisely as the *Alma-nac's* left-handed calendar pages said it would. The calendar page also showed that the 27-day-old moon had left Leo and was entering Virgo. Noted on the right-handed calendar pages were the facts that on this date in 1743, a storm blocked Ben Franklin's view of a lunar eclipse and that, besides election day, Tuesday also marked the 125th anniversary of Tchaikovsky's death. The weather prediction rhyme for the week read, "Dank and dismal, drearie. Just short of abysmal." This—while managing to be both cryptic and obvious—was also very true, since there'd been heavy rain and wind much of the week-end. Planning ahead, it was predicted that on Thursday "Black bears head to winter dens now." On the following Tuesday, "Lobsters move to offshore waters." And the forecast for two weeks hence: "Crab apples are ripe now."

In this way, the old-fashioned *Almanac* was a perfect companion piece to Franklin County Cider Days. It's the oldest and most important cider festival in the Northeast, but it's a rather humble affair, centered around the historic Western Massachusetts towns of Greenfield, Deerfield, and Turners Falls, just down the road from the Yankee Candle factory. Most of the events are free—demonstrations for home cider makers, seminars on pruning and tending to apple trees, and family orchard tours. Enthusiasts crowd into tasting rooms at local cideries such as Bear Swamp Orchard and Cidery and Headwater Cider Company. I visited West County Cider, which started in 1984, making it one of the oldest American cideries of the contemporary era. There, under a tent next to a roaring fire pit, I tasted single-variety ciders made from Esopus Spitzenburg and Reine des Pommes and a pink cider made from all Redfield red-fleshed apples, which were discovered by West County's founder, the late Terry Maloney, who also co-created Cider Days. This rosé, West County's bestseller, was more complex than most of Big Cider's drink-pink offerings, including Angry Orchard's.

On Friday night, there was a Cider Schmooze in the basement bar of a local performing arts center, as well as a Cider Sing at the local Episcopal church's parish hall, where people sat in a circle sharing cider and singing songs like "Comfort me with apples / Shake them from the tree / Taste the sweet and sparkling juice / Cider for me."

On the Saturday evening, I joined the crowds under a tent in the village park of Turners Falls for the Cider Salon, where four dozen producers from around the country, as well as from Europe, poured their finest ciders—possibly the largest tasting of the cider season.

Aaron Burr and Angry Orchard had come from upstate New York, as well as other producers such as Albemarle CiderWorks from Virginia, Anxo Cidery from Washington, DC, Stem Ciders from Colorado, Tandem Ciders from Michigan, and Tilted Shed Ciderworks from California. But it was the contingent from New England that was most evident: Farnum Hill from New Hampshire; Eden, Stowe Cider, and Fable Farm from Vermont; Urban Farm Fermentory and Cornish Cider Company from Maine; Carr's Ciderhouse, Far From The Tree Cider, and Stormalong from Massachusetts. The New England cideries also provided the evening's corniest apple puns on labels like Stormalong's Mass Appeal, Far From the Tree's Apple of My Chai, and Stowe Cider's Pippin Ain't Easy.

* * *

This was my second November at Cider Days. The year before, I'd attended an amazing talk, "A History of Apples in America," given by a man named John Bunker. This was at Bear Swamp Orchards, a half hour from Greenfield, where about 50 people crowded inside the cidery, seated on folding chairs amid tanks and barrels, sipping little plastic cups of cider.

Bunker, a native Mainer, has spent nearly five decades hunting and preserving forgotten apple varieties in New England. He is revered in orchard circles for his Fedco Trees Annual Catalog for Spring Planting, a prime source for cider apple trees in the Northeast, with about 70 apple varieties listed for sale, from Ashmead's Kernel to Calville Blanc d'Hiver to Hewe's Virginia Crab to Ribston Pippin to Zestar. It even lists Eric Shatt's Gnarled Chapman that he cultivated from wild seedling. "Not every apple is right for you," says the catalog. "If you don't eat many apples fresh but love pies, go for the pie apples. If you're a dessert connoisseur, skip all others and go for the highly flavored dessert varieties. Some are strictly for cider. Some are great to put out at the camp for summer use. Some are perfect for those who want fall fruit but don't have a root cellar."

But beyond shopping and advice, the Fedco Trees annual catalog is a delightful literary work in and of itself, full of homespun illustrations and small, joyful sidebars on apple growing, history, and even reading recommendations from "Bunker's Bookshelf." You might find a how-to on grafting, a capsule review of William Coxe's 1817 book, *A View of the Cultivation of Fruit Trees*, and short profiles of Russian botanist Nikolai Vavilov ("Hero of biological diversity") or groundbreaking 19th-century botanist Kate Furbush ("Maine's Dauntless Plant Explorer") or 19th-century Quaker minister/farmer Joseph Taylor ("Champion of the chance seedling"). There is, naturally, a sidebar about John "Appleseed" Chapman. The Fedco catalog grows out of a similar nostalgic tradition as the *Old Farmer's Almanac* and certainly falls under the *Almanac's* motto: "Useful, with a pleasant degree of humor."

With a graying goatee and wearing a baseball cap and jean jacket, the 67-year-old Bunker began his talk by saying, "Baldwin, I consider to be the most historical apple in America." But there was a lot of ground to cover before we got to the Baldwin. First, he referenced Thoreau's "Wild Apples" essay and talked about the apple's heterozygosity, how each apple planted from seed is different. "It doesn't matter if they have the same mom and dad," he said. "All of us resemble our mother and our father, but we're not replicants. We are all unique. Every one of us is like an apple."

In fact, Bunker insisted, "The whole history of us is in these apples." He talked about how wild apples existed in New England long before the Pilgrims arrived and the Massachusetts Bay Colony was created. But the Native Americans in that region did not eat apples, and so how they got here is a mystery. "We think it might have been Basque fishermen, long before the 17th century," Bunker said. It makes sense, since Basque fishing ships in the 16th century were built to carry huge barrels in their hulls, filled with cider from the vast orchards back home around present-day San Sebastián. Basque sailors had a reputation in those days as the strongest and hardiest, in part because of the vast amounts of cider they consumed, which kept scurvy away. Still, historians have no conclusive evidence and so the Basque connection, for now, is only a theory. In any case, by the mid-1600s, wild apples thrived in Massachusetts alongside the European varieties brought by early settlers.

Before long, the settlers began making selections of which seedlings to graft and cultivate, to cut down on the uncertainty of growing apples from seedling. It's believed that the Roxbury Russet was the first selected apple variety. It makes sense, since russet apples have thick, rough skins and were useful for settlers. "Russets became popular because you could store them in a hole in the ground through the winter," Bunker said. You can still find plenty of ciders in the Northeast with Roxbury Russet in the blend.

By 1636, the Puritan minister Roger Williams was booted out of the Massachusetts Bay Colony for "sedition and heresy" and moved with his followers to Rhode Island. In 1650, a green apple called the Rhode Island Greening was discovered in the village of Green's End (near modern-day Newport) from a tree found behind the inn of a tavern keeper named Green. "All the original apple names were a method of keeping track of what you had and from where," Bunker said. "They were not marketing opportunities. There was no Honeycrisp or SnapDragon." The Rhode Island Greening quickly became one of the most popular apples in early America. "They eventually took so many twigs off the original tree that they killed it." But the apple lived on in scores of other orchards, and the Rhode Island Greening is still found today in many heritage ciders.

Finally, Bunker got to the history of the Baldwin apple, which was discovered in Massachusetts, along the proposed route for the Middlesex Canal in the 1740s. The Baldwin didn't get its official name, however, until 1795. "Up until then, they were calling it a Pecker, short for 'woodpecker,' because the tree was liked by woodpeckers," Bunker told us. With the advent of commercial orchards, the Baldwin—along with the Roxbury Russet and Rhode Island Greening—became "the most important apples in America for 150 years," right up until the Civil War. The original tree died in 1815, knocked over by a gale; a monument now stands at the site in present-day Wilmington, Massachusetts.

At that point, Bunker regaled us with stories about other apples, such as the Yellow Bellflower, found in 1817. "This is a New Jersey apple," he said. "We don't hold that against it." He held up a Black Oxford, "This is a Maine apple. You can see its beautiful color. It's a keeper, meaning you can keep it all winter." As Bunker was just starting in apples as a young man, he said he'd go to orchardist meetings and hear people say, "These old varieties, they're terrible. They should cut them all down. They're spitters." But he wondered why other people insisted on growing them, eventually realizing that the apples people grew in the old days were meant for pies or cider, never to be eaten out of hand. "So I decided that if I wanted to understand why people kept these apples, I should learn how to make a pie," he said. "So I made pies with every variety. And I made apple sauce with every variety." He sought out 19th-century cookbooks. "For pies, you have to have an apple that will cook in exactly one hour. You don't want it to turn to soup or into worn rubber." Roxbury Russet, he said, was the best for winter apple sauce.

At that point, Bunker grew wistful as he spoke about the terrible winter of 1934. "It was so terrible that tens of millions of apple trees in New England and New York were killed," he said. "There was an

80-degree drop in temperature in one 24-hour period. Old-timers say you could walk into the woods and hear trees exploding." With sadness in his voice as if this had happened yesterday and not eight decades ago, Bunker said, "The orchard industry in New England never recovered."

I had never heard about the devastating winter of 1934, and later followed up to find that February 1934 was indeed the coldest month ever recorded in Boston, with an average temperature of 17.5 degrees and the coldest-ever recorded temperature, at minus-18. Boston meteorologist Eric Fisher calls February 1934 "the gold standard for cold." But what strikes me most is that this would have been the winter following the repeal of Prohibition, on December 5, 1933. It's often repeated that "Prohibition killed off cider apples." But the notion of temperance movement activists violently chopping down trees is overblown. There's little evidence that this was a widespread campaign. More likely, cider apples disappeared more quietly, with farmers replanting orchards with dessert apples that they could actually sell, or simply abandoning the cider orchards altogether. Bunker's suggestion that the deep winter freeze was a bigger reason for the die-off of cider apple trees, many of which had been neglected during the 13 years of Prohibition, makes more sense.

When the talk ended, Bunker served us West County Cider that was made with 100 percent Baldwins, and set a pile of the crimson-and yellow-streaked apples on a table. "If you want a Baldwin, come up and get one," he said.

* * *

I loved Bunker's talk, and since I spent my late teens and early twenties in Vermont and Boston, the whole Yankee New England shtick has always been near and dear to my heart. The aesthetic, tradition—and above all, the history—are some of the great appeals of cider for me. But I realize that's not the case for everyone. As cider continues to grow, there's a sense, especially among younger cider people, that too much emphasis has been placed on history and tradition in promoting the beverage to consumers. Some even object to the term *heritage* ciders. On their Redfield Radio cider podcast, hosts Olivia Maki and Mike Reis, who own a cider bar and bottle shop in Oakland, California, often talk about how the cider industry is homogenous or "hella white" and how they're uncomfortable with some of the connotations of the word *heritage*. "Heritage just makes me feel a little icky," Reis said in one episode. "It just doesn't have that much of a connection to today's cider makers, even if a lot of cider makers like to embrace that old-timey image in their marketing." (Reis and Maki prefer the term "orchard-based" ciders, which is a little reductive since even crappy apples for juice concentrate come from orchards.)

Even Dan Pucci, the pommelier formerly of Wassail, has published a series of essays in *Malus* warning against the nostalgia marketing of cider. "We must be skeptical of building cider on a foundation of nostalgia," he writes. Pucci argues that too many articles, blog posts, podcasts, and sales pitches talk about cider in terms of early American history and the Founding Fathers. Not just John Adams and his tankard a day and Ben Franklin and his Newtown Pippins, but also Thomas Jefferson planting cider apples at Monticello and George Washington campaigning by serving hundreds of gallons of cider. Then there's the whole Johnny Appleseed thing.

Pucci's solution is to focus on apple variety, terroir, and vintage—to align cider more closely with conversations people have about wine. In fact, on the Sunday afternoon after I browsed the *Old Farmer's Almanac*, I attended a Cider Days presentation by Pucci and writer Darlene Hayes in which they poured a half-dozen ciders made with 100 percent Newtown Pippin, all from different places—from New York's Finger Lakes to Albemarle County, Virginia, to Sonoma County, California, to New Zealand. They even provided slices of the specific apples used in each cider. Though the venue for this tasting was the historic community center in the quintessentially Yankee town of Deerfield (settled 1673), this was a thoroughly contemporary connoisseur experience.

"Nostalgia serves to speculate on what might have been, rather than what could be," Pucci writes in his *Malus* essay. "The narrative does not serve cider in the long term." Even in mid-19th-century America, cider represented an idealized, nostalgic—sometimes reactionary—past. Pucci points to William Henry Harrison, who ran a divisive, populist campaign for president as the self-proclaimed "log cabin and hard cider candidate." By 1840, the Industrial Revolution was in full swing; cider, and the farming tradition it grew from, was already on the decline. Cider became a charged political symbol of the common man's desire for simpler times. The Whig Party seized on this and presented Harrison in opposition to the "elite" Martin Van Buren, who presided over the Panic of 1837, the nation's first major financial crisis, banking collapse, and recession. Van Buren was depicted on campaign flyers as a Champagne-drinking wine snob who recoiled at the taste of cider. The complete opposite was actually true, with the irony being that Harrison was born into one of the wealthiest (and slave-owning) families in Virginia. Regardless, the Whigs stoked populist anger, and Harrison won the presidency. (He died 31 days into office, of pneumonia, allegedly because he didn't wear a top hat or overcoat to his inauguration in freezing weather.)

The parallels between the "log cabin and hard cider" 1840 campaign and more recent election promises to "Make America Great Again" are perhaps too close for comfort, as Pucci notes: "Today, right-wing populism plays upon the same insecurity as the Whig Party was able to co-opt in 1840. The Trump White House has exploited a narrative of American nostalgia to pursue their agenda, often at the cost of the interests of their own supporters." The difference now, Pucci insists, is that cider represents the opposite: a "progressive nature" that "exudes democratic (with a small d) social, cultural, and political values."

Pucci's connection of cider and Trump and dangerously nostalgic ideas about America struck me deeply. During the first fall season of my own cider journey, Trump and cider were heavily entwined in my own mind. Not that Trump wasn't on everyone's mind all the time. But for me, literally in between my visits to cideries and orchards, I'd been traveling to Trump vacation properties around the world for a long, dystopian feature I wrote for the *Washington Post Magazine*. My trips to the Finger Lakes bookended travel to the Trump golf resort in Aberdeen, Scotland, and the abandoned former Trump casinos in Atlantic City. A trip to Vermont was followed immediately by a trip to the eerie near-emptiness and peeling paint of the Trump Tower in Panama. I visited cideries in Virginia while I stayed at the Trump Winery. A visit to the Pacific Northwest included a side trip to the Trump International Hotel & Tower in Vancouver.

I didn't go to these Trump properties as an investigative journalist or political commentator, simply as a travel writer. By then, Trump had been dissected in nearly every other genre: politics, entertainment, finance, fashion, sports. Why not look at Trump through the prism of travel writing? So I slept in the various Trump hotels, experienced the Trump amenities, ate and drank in the Trump restaurants and bars. I believed it would be no different from when I anonymously visit and review any other establishment in the course of an article. This, of course, was totally naive. As a jaded travel writer, someone who's stayed in many soulless hotels and eaten in many overpriced restaurants in many disappointing places, I'm completely at ease with a certain exquisite idleness and ennui. But there was something profoundly unsettling about the sort of boredom that I'd felt in the Trump properties over many weeks.

As one tiny example of the insistent overhyping and under-delivering, consider the gold-lettered plaque that stands near the clubhouse of the Trump golf course in Aberdeen, Scotland (where you could eat something called "haggis bonbons" with "whisky mayonnaise"). This plaque memorializes the opening of this course "conceived and built by Donald J. Trump" (in 2012) as if it were an official historic site. It reads:

> Encompassing the world's largest dunes, The Great Dunes of Scotland, Mr. Trump and his architect, Dr. Martin Hawtree, delicately wove these magnificent golf holes through this unparalleled 600 acre site running along the majestic North Sea. The unprecedented end result is, according to many, the greatest golf course anywhere in the world!

So many mistruths to unpack on one plaque. To take just the first line, the so-called "Great Dunes" are in reality part of an environmentally sensitive area called the Sands of Forvie (which Trump bulldozed) and these dunes are nowhere close to the "world's largest"—South America and Africa have dunes five or more times taller. The Sands of Forvie is only the fifth-largest dune system in Britain. And the golf course is nowhere near the "greatest." A recent ranking in *Golf Digest* lists it as the world's 54th best course.

My respite from the relentless, in-your-face mediocrity of Trump World was returning to cider country, where I could once again put on my muddy boots and a flannel shirt and walk the orchards. Drinking what is classified as heritage cider—as opposed to mass-market modern cider—kept me sane.

Only a few days before I went to Massachusetts to experience my first Cider Days and hear Bunker's talk on the history of apples, I found myself after dark in Vancouver's downtown financial district gazing up at the twisting, neo-futurist Trump International Hotel & Tower, rising 62 stories and 616 feet into the air. That's pretty tall, but across the street is the Living Shangri-La tower, also rising 62 stories, but standing 659 feet tall. Which made me chuckle because that meant Trump, a man obsessed with superlatives, has his name emblazoned on the *second*-tallest building in Vancouver.

The magazine paid almost $300 per night for me to stay in one of the tower's five-star hotel rooms. After I checked in, I tried on the robe embroidered with "TRUMP," along with the TRUMP-branded shower cap, in my marble-tiled bathroom. I was given a very professional, very invigorating massage treatment at The Spa by Ivanka Trump™ (which "personifies her lifestyle, embarking on every endeavor with energy and passion, but always taking the time to pause, heal, and recharge"). At the spa, a woman asked me about my "intention" for today's treatment. "Calm, restore, or energize?" she asked. Frankly, the whole notion of my "intention" had been nagging at me, existentially, for weeks.

That night in Vancouver I would have dinner at Mott 32, the "luxury Chinese" spot on the ground floor of the Trump Hotel. As I was about to step inside the hotel, a black SUV cruised past with its passenger window down. A young woman leaned out, waving two middle fingers and screaming at the top of her lungs: "Fuck you, Trump! Fuck you! Fuck you! Fuck you, Trump!" I was one of only two people standing outside the entrance, and so it felt like all of her hate was directed at me. Since I seemed to be a paying customer at a Trump resort, I guessed that was her point. After the SUV cruised on, the street was quiet again. A Trump employee standing nearby shrugged and opened the lobby door for me, his body language similar to the bartender I chatted with at the Trump Champagne Lounge earlier, who grimaced when the name "Donald Trump" was uttered.

At Mott 32, I sat at the bar and watched a waiter carve a $95 Peking duck, not even close to the most expensive dish on the menu: A whole suckling pig cost $495; braised whole dried fish maw, in abalone sauce, was listed at $580. Looking at the drinks list, I was surprised to see a section for "Craft Cider." There were familiar cider producers, like Normandy's Christian Drouin, and a few unfamiliar local bottles from British Columbia. I ordered a $15 (Canadian) glass of Manoir du Kinkiz, from Brittany, France, which the menu described as "ultra dry, rustic tannins, bruised apple flesh, pumpkin seeds." By the bottle, the price was $69 Canadian.

I ordered a few of the more affordable small dishes from the "Evening Dim Sum" menu: a middling duck spring roll, some hot-and-sour Shanghai-style soup dumplings, which were surprisingly tasty, and a disappointing black truffle siu mai with pork and a soft-boiled quail egg, served at room temperature. The bartender made a little joke when he served the siu mai: "Be careful about the egg inside. It's a soft yolk and you don't want it all over your shirt."

He suggested a local offering from Fraser Valley Cider Company, apparently made with English and French cider apples, and described on the menu as "juicy, mouthwatering, apricot, white flowers, golden apples." It was also $15 Canadian per glass. This was heritage cider in a very unlikely context. I told the bartender about the screaming protester who'd driven by outside, and he looked pained. "Ah, politics," he said. "I have friends that tell me, 'Well, we can't visit you now because you work at that place.'"

Later that night, alone in my Trump-branded hotel room, watching reports about the Mueller investigation on CNN, I thought about the experience of drinking high-priced ciders in a luxury Chinese restaurant on the ground floor of the Trump Tower. Was this what cider looked like completely unlinked from nostalgia and history? If so, what did that even mean? I also thought about the woman earlier in the evening who screamed from her SUV, yelling at those of us who happened to be standing outside the cold, glistening tower. It may have been a bit over the top, but I deeply understood the rage behind it. I realized that what terrifies me is not that Trump's presidency will end up as an exploding, burning disaster, one capable of inspiring white-hot outrage and hysteria—but rather as something dangerously lukewarm. Sort of like that middling black truffle siu mai with boiled quail egg inside, served room temperature, with the soft yolk that threatens to ooze down your shirt. I also thought about how that siu mai paired with heritage cider and whether politics and cider should mix at all. And then I fell asleep.

CHAPTER 6

"NEW HAMPSHIRE IS A STATE.
VERMONT IS A BRAND."

For more than a decade, in my various writings on booze, I have been recommending that my readers drink Farnum Hill cider. Made in New Hampshire, these were the first American ciders I found that came bottled like wine, were made with real cider apples, were consistently dry, and could rival or surpass what was imported from Europe. In particular, Farnum Hill's Extra Dry blend and single-varietal Kingston Black are classics. Oddly enough, though, I'd never visited founders Steve Wood and Louisa Spencer at their Poverty Lane Orchards. Many cider makers across the country, from New York to Virginia to Michigan to the West Coast, told me about their debt to Wood, for his guidance and advice—and especially for the scion wood he'd given them. Dozens of cider orchards have been established with cuttings from Wood's Dabinetts, Yarlington Mills, Chisel Jerseys, Wickson Crabs, Kingston Blacks, and others.

I contacted Wood and told him that I wanted to stop by to talk about the cider revival. In less than an hour, Wood rang my cell phone. In a big booming voice, he said, "I want you to know that I didn't mean to be the guy who caused all these Dabinett apples to be grown all over the US. I didn't mean to be the godfather. We're giving away budwood all over the country. But I always ask, 'Do you know if this will grow where you live?' Because I sure as fuck don't know." Wood also wanted to let me know he was an orchardist, and didn't want to hear about "this new fad" of people foraging for wild apples.

"In Bordeaux, do they run out into the woods in the fall to pick wild grapes?" he said. "No. Long ago, they chose to cultivate and focus on cabernet sauvignon and merlot."

Lebanon, New Hampshire, is about an hour and a half north of Greenfield, Massachusetts, up Interstate 91 along the Connecticut River, just across the border from Vermont. I arrived at Poverty Lane Orchards one beautiful evening as the sun was setting over the brilliant foliage and the last customers at the orchard for Pick Your Own apples were just settling up.

Wood already awaited me inside the cidery, manically pouring samples from beakers and flasks into wine glasses. "We're making scary organoleptic decisions here," he said. He was testing a new blend for Farnum Hill's flagship Farmhouse cider, with samples from the previous fall's vintage that had been aging for a year. I asked how many apples were in the blend. "I don't know," he said. "13? 22?" Wood insisted he was committed to blends over single-varietal bottlings. "Every great cider apple, like the best wine grape, is still missing something," he said. "So why bottle them by themselves? They want to play together."

They'd settled on a house style for blends like Farmhouse and Extra Dry back in the late 1990s and early 2000s, but Wood felt it was time to tweak things. "Farmhouse has always been our cheap and cheerful," he said. But Wood could see that cider enthusiasts' tastes were rapidly changing. "For a while we started to turn down the tannins on Farmhouse," he said. "But lately we've gotten some lukewarm reviews, where the reviewers say it's not in-your-face enough. So now I want to bring out the bittersweet quality more. I want to turn up the tannins." It's the opposite of ten years ago, he said. "People used to say it was too dry and tannic!"

Changing the blend of Farmhouse wasn't the only new development happening at Farnum Hill. A new $750,000 cidery would soon be built, ready for the fall of 2018. This was also a change that concerned Wood. "We've made a lot of good cider out of this space," he said, waving his arms around what is a converted old barn.

Wood's wife, Louise Spencer—whom everyone calls LouLou—joined us, and we went to dinner at an Italian trattoria on the surprisingly bustling main square in Lebanon, which is close to Hanover, the home of Dartmouth University. Wood and Spencer are like royalty in Lebanon (Wood served on the city council for years), and the restaurant owner made a big fuss when we walked in. "I think when this place opened it was the first time I saw a pair of leather pants in Lebanon," Spencer said.

Over dinner, Wood ranted about his status as the godfather or elder statesman of the cider revival. "I do not want to be anyone's guru. I shouldn't be," he said. "We don't even know what we're doing here. We have actively tried to dissuade people from starting an apple orchard."

When I asked how they got started, Spencer said, "Well, we didn't just call up some guy in New Hampshire and ask for budwood."

Poverty Lane Orchards was started as a "gentleman's orchard" by Wood's father, who was the town doctor in Lebanon. "He probably delivered 2,800 babies," Wood said. As a boy in the 1960s, Wood worked at the orchard. "When I was 11, these trees were the size of my thumb, and I was spreading mulch with a pitchfork," he said. After going off to college at Harvard in the 1970s, he eventually returned and devoted his life to apple growing. In 1984 he bought the farm to run himself. At first, he sold dessert fruit, but then prices for fresh apples crashed. "Back in 1979, people paid a premium for the quality of McIntosh. By the late 1980s, the premium for our Macs evaporated," he said. That was when cheap Granny Smith apples from the Southern Hemisphere flooded the market. "People said, 'Oh, look, a fresh apple in the spring!'"

Around that time, Wood and Spencer were traveling in England and visited the traditional cider region of Herefordshire. "There were all these weird fucking orchards there," he said. They were filled with strange, ugly apples you didn't want to eat. But that was when Wood had an epiphany: They would rip out the dessert apples and plant English cider apples instead. Poverty Lane Orchards now grows dozens of these varieties.

"We spent a decade or more doing grafting trials to try to figure out which varieties would work well around here," he said. Now Wood and Spencer own orchards spanning more than 75 acres, with 20,000 trees. "We are the biggest grower of inedible apples," Wood joked— and, until recently, they were indeed the largest producer of bittersweet apples in the country. Besides making their own cider, Poverty Lane Orchards supplies apples to Big Cider companies like Angry Orchard down to artisan operations that make a few hundred cases.

"How do you start a cider orchard?" Wood said. He threw a knife on the table next to the plates of pasta. "That's the magic wand right there. You graft a tree and then you watch it grow for two to three years. You're looking at four years before you get something faintly significant, and eight years before you get any volume. This is not art, this is work. If I'm cocky about anything, it's that I know I can grow an apple. And if I've learned anything about apples for cider, it's this: You want them ripe."

As for the cider, after much trial and error, Wood and Spencer had another epiphany in the late 1990s. "We started smelling and tasting things we only could get from what we grew here," Wood said. "We realized we could make American—and not English or French—cider. But I want to be clear that neither of us knew what the hell we were doing."

After dinner, Spencer went home to bed, leaving Wood and me at the cidery barn to drink some more. I asked if we could taste some of the Kingston Black, telling him that it's always been one of my favorite ciders. Wood grumbled, but grabbed a bottle of Kingston Black, poured it into my glass, and said: "I'm so tired of fussy ciders like this!" He told me, "I don't what to hear any of this pretentious wine talk. We don't want anyone doing that with cider."

I told him I thought he should make more single-varietal ciders. He reminded me that he had a knife in his pocket. We finished the bottle of Kingston Black and opened another.

* * *

In the morning, I was to meet Wood again at the cidery to taste more samples of the new Farmhouse blend, as well as to take a tour of his orchards. I arrived very early, and wandered the rows of trees in the Pick-Your-Own orchard in the misty morning. The day before, I'd been given a stapled packet with varieties listed by row and tree number. So I was the clichéd kid in the candy store, following the numbers and grabbing and biting into varieties I'd never before tasted: Hewe's Virginia Crab, St. Edmund's Pippin, Sweet Alford, Pomme Grise, Westfield Seek-No-Further, Hubbardston Nonesuch. As I crunched through my rare-apple breakfast, I stood listening to the sounds of the orchard: the rustle of leaves, the squawk of birds, and the occasional thump of an apple hitting the ground.

When I returned to the cidery, Wood was there with his team. They showed me a new canned cider about to launch—the first time Farnum Hill would be sold in a can. This would be part of a collaboration called Cider Grown with Eden Specialty Ciders from Vermont and Stormalong Cider from Massachusetts. Each of these New England producers would have a can in the four-pack, with the fourth cider being a combination of all three producers' juice.

Wood said he'd put a lot of early ripening bittersweet apples in the Farnum Hill. I cracked it open, and there were big pineapple and celery aromas and it was dry and easy-drinking, a cider for a summer day after mowing the lawn. The others were much sweeter. I was a little thrown by why Farnum Hill would want to release a can like this, especially as part of a rather random mixed four-pack. After all, they'd been the pioneers who showed everyone that cider could be poured like wine from 750-mililiter bottles and not a draft line. Why would they mingle their juice with anyone else's?

The rest of the Farnum Hill team had now gathered and it was time to taste some sample blends for the new Farmhouse. Wood and I joined Nicole Leibon, the head cider maker, Wanda Loynds, a manager, and Spencer. "Tart acid, stone fruit, and the bitter's got some quinine," Leibon said of the first sample.

"I get grapefruit peel. And does anyone else get pineapple?" Spencer said.

"I get mango," Loynds said. "I also get something kelpy. Seaweed? Like something lying on a beach."

Leibon wrote down everyone's impressions of the samples. "Don't forget my mango," Loynds said. "Also, on the finish I get pine nut and witch hazel."

Sample two was described as "dried apricot and tangerine," "gardenia and seltzer," and "orange blossoms and pecans." Sample three was described variously as "chamomile," "marmalade," and "brandy." Loynds said, "Honestly, this smells like human sweat after a big night of drinking."

All of this sounded curiously similar to what Wood had called "pretentious wine talk" the night before.

After the tasting, Wood and I drove up to some of his orchards, about 15 minutes away, and climbed to around 800 feet in elevation. I asked if apple trees could grow on a mountaintop. "Apples trees will grow anywhere," he said. A little further down the road, I asked him if Poverty Lane Orchards was organic. "We are not organic," he said. "We are aggressively not organic."

When we finally arrived at the orchard, he said, "This orchard has had a hard life. The trees have been mutilated by porcupines. Porcupines are horrible. They're drawn to high pH fruit. I'm a fucking genius. I bring all these varieties over from England, where they have no porcupines." As we walked, he pulled a handgun out of his bag. "That's why I carry this. We've killed 140 porcupines in this field." All I could think about was New Hampshire's state motto, emblazoned on its license plates: "Live Free or Die."

We walked through rows of Dabinett, the crimson-red bittersweet from Somerset, England, that Wood is perhaps best known for cultivating. He picked one off the ground. "Now this one's ripe," he said. He grabbed one from the tree. "Now bite this one."

"It's like bitter water," I said.

"More like bitter water with a potato in it," he said. "We want the starches to turn into sugar."

I happened to refer to the ripe apples on the ground as "drops" and Wood said, "Drops? This is $25 a fucking bushel."

We finally reached the place where Wood's crew was picking and loading a trailer pulled by a tractor. Most of the eight men were from Jamaica, annual migrant laborers. In fact, it's common to see Jamaicans picking apples at large commercial orchards all over the Northeast. Wood told me that Fitz, his crew chief, has worked with him for 25 years, and lives in Lebanon year-round. "My sons grew up on his shoulders," Wood said. "When I was a kid, if a black guy walked down the street in Lebanon, it would have been talked about at the diner. Not now."

Wood told his crew, "The ones on the ground are ripe. The ones on the trees are not. I've been biting them all the way down the row."

The men began gathering the apples off the ground, with a steady, thump, thump, thump into their buckets. One guy started singing a sort of old-timey, a cappella folk song.

We drove back down from the orchard and turned onto Maxfield Parrish Highway. We started talking about the difference between New Hampshire and Vermont, which is only a few minutes away across the Connecticut River. "New Hampshire is a state," he said. "Vermont is a brand." I laughed and he said, "I'm serious! New Hampshire has a serious industrial history. Vermont does not."

Wood continued, "The Industrial Revolution happened in this region. There were textile mills, tanneries, quarries, all kinds of industry. Those things were just closing when I was a kid. In 1965 the middle of Lebanon burned down. There were a lot of tough neighborhoods around here."

Was cider part of that history? I asked. "Ha, I don't fucking know. Two-thirds of cider history is apocryphal. I have no fucking idea what people drank back then."

A few more miles down the road, after some twists and turns, he pointed out a one-room schoolhouse. This is the kind of romantic New England thing I'm a sucker for—covered bridges, old red barns, one-room schoolhouses. This is what I'd actually been hoping to find at Farnum Hill. Excitedly, I asked Wood: "Did you go to school there?"

"Ha, are you kidding me?" he said, with a laugh. "How old do you fucking think I am?"

* * *

As I drove into Vermont later that day, I was deep in thought about what Wood had said: Vermont is a brand. I'd gone to school two decades ago at the University of Vermont, in Burlington, and after a long time away, I'd been rekindling my relationship with the state in recent years. I'd written articles about Vermont's artisan cheese makers, its maple syrup industry, and its craft beer scene. I'd been told that Vermont was like "the Napa Valley of cheese" as well as "the Napa Valley of craft beer." After a tasting of maple syrups, it was suggested that Vermont might also be "the Napa Valley of maple syrup." So it did not surprise me at all when Colin Davis, the co-founder of Shacksbury Cider, suggested that the state "could be like the Napa Valley of hard cider." I was fairly ambivalent about the idea of Vermont's becoming "the Napa Valley" of anything. The Vermont I remember from college in the early 1990s was a weird, groovy place that's close to my heart. It's sort of the last place I would have believed would latch on to the wine-ification of everything. But I know that's probably naive. I realized that Vermont had become a very different place.

What I was not ambivalent about was that I did not like the idea of cider closely following the craft beer model, with all its hype, gimmicky experiments, and manufactured scarcity of trendy, limited-edition releases. I'd traveled around Vermont with my brother Tyler a couple of years earlier on a craft beer tour. And by craft beer tour, I mean that we drove 400 miles to stand in line at various cult breweries. Consider our visit to The Alchemist brewery in Stowe as a cautionary tale for cider.

We arrived at The Alchemist at 9:45 A.M. on a freezing morning, but the parking lot was closed with a sign that read "Parking Lot Opens at 10 A.M. . . . Please Do Not Arrive Early." An employee politely but firmly suggested we go get some coffee and come back in 15 minutes. When we returned at 10:02, we were the 10th car in line. "Do you think you should jump out and get in line?" I asked.

"Are you kidding me?" Tyler replied. "The brewery doesn't even open until 11!" Once we finally got into line, we stood numbers 18 and 19, I could see at least 40 more people shivering behind us. In front of us was a bearded guy who wore a furry earflap hat and had sprinted from his car carrying a cooler. The bearded guy in front of us unfastened his earflaps and chuckled at Tyler's annoyance and string of obscenities. "Haven't you guys ever stood in line for beer before?" he asked.

"No," Tyler said. "Never."

"They said there was a line around the parking lot the other day," said the earflap guy. He'd driven up that morning from near Boston, four hours away. This wasn't his first time in line at The Alchemist. "So are you guys maxing out your purchases?"

"What do you mean?" I asked.

"You're only allowed to buy 10 four-packs of Heady and the others."

By Heady, he meant Heady Topper, the almost-mythic double India pale ale that The Alchemist brews. Heady Topper has scored a perfect 100 from BeerAdvocate, where readers have in years past rated it the top beer in the world (it's always in the top 10). Heady Topper is sold mostly in limited production, delivered on specific days to be released at specific times in specific stores, where it sells out in minutes. Beer geeks know which days and times Heady is delivered to small-town general stores and routinely make six-, eight- or 10-hour drives to buy it.

"The line's bigger today because of Petit Mutant," said the earflap guy. "They're releasing that today."

Finally, an employee stepped outside and addressed the crowd. "Today, we're offering PUH-teet Mooo-*tahnt*," he said, pronouncing "petit" in American English but "mutant" in a sort of pretentious French-ish accent. He told us that Petit Mutant is a wild ale fermented with Brettanomyces yeast, as well as "about a pound and a half of cherries per bottle," and that "all the cherries are from

Vermont." He also told us we would be able to buy only one bottle per person.

As we snaked through the line, we were poured sample beers, and for about 18 minutes the line puttered along. These hazy, high-alcohol, unfiltered IPAs are the prototypical Vermont- or New England–style IPAs, the controversial style that took the craft beer world by storm not too long ago. I asked Tyler, "What did you think of the famous Heady Topper?"

"It's a hazy, high-alcohol double IPA," he said. "It's fine, but I can't understand what all this fuss is about."

"Well," I said. "Critics say it's the best beer in the world."

He looked at me skeptically. "Who? Who judged it the best? That's what I want to know."

When we finally got to the cashier, we bought two bottles of Petit Mutant and a few four-packs of the other beers. Tyler bought some IPA-scented lip balm. We forked over $90. Then, we exited The Alchemist. (*Don't let the door hit you on the ass!*) That was the entire experience. In the parking lot, grown men were literally running to their cars to deposit their purchases and then running to get back in line to buy more.

Now, a couple of years later, as I drove through the gorgeous, multihued Green Mountains fall landscape, I worried again about cider following the craft beer path, taking its cues from breweries. The fact that Farnum Hill was now canning cider, for instance, alarmed me. I'm certainly not against cider in cans, but I worry about the message it sends to potential consumers. Though I guess many of these consumers want cider in cans, which is why the cideries sell cider in cans to begin with? This kind of thinking makes my head hurt.

* * *

To be clear, there are a bunch of great cideries in Vermont. Flag Hill Farm Cyder, with its high-elevation cider-apple orchard in Vershire, started in the same era as Farnum Hill and as West County in Massachusetts. Fable Farm Fermentory in South Royalton has been warmly embraced by natural wine lovers. Newcomer Tin Hat Cider, in Roxbury, is an excellent small producer to watch. Teddy Weber, a musician who once played in the blues and ragtime band the Wiyos, now forages wild apples and has planted an orchard on his forested property. At 1,800 feet above sea level, he grows Dabinett, Kingston Black, and Medaille d'Or from scion wood he got at Farnum Hill. I discovered bottles of Tin Hat in a small shop in the ski village of Stowe, also the home of The Alchemist. "I'm surrounded by Heady Topper and Lawson's Sip of Sunshine up here!" Weber told me. "Everyone is jumping on the can bandwagon because of craft beer. But that's not how I want to enjoy my cider."

In the dead of winter, I visited Eden Specialty Ciders, in Vermont's Northeast Kingdom, near the Canadian border. Eden makes all manner of cider, from still to Champagne-method to even a semi-dry canned cider. But the stars of the show are Eleanor Léger's acclaimed ice ciders. Ice ciders are a curious subcategory, made by concentrating the juice, either by freezing the fruit before pressing, or freezing the fresh-pressed juice and then drawing off the concentrated juice as it thaws. The fermentation is often stopped before dryness so that it retains a good amount of residual sugar. The end result, for Eden, is a sweet nectar that's comparable to Sauternes or other coveted dessert wines. At Cider Days, Léger poured her 2007 Falstaff ice cider, and it was so complex it was almost like a rare palo cortado sherry.

By law, true ice cider can only be made by outdoor freezing and not artificial refrigeration. So there are very few places in the US with the sustained below-freezing temperature where ice cider can be made. In fact, there is more of a tradition farther north in Quebec. But it certainly gets cold enough in Vermont's Northeast Kingdom. On the day I visited Léger in February, it snowed more than two feet. "The freezing is the easy part," Léger said. "The whole trick is crashing the fermentation at the right moment."

But the first cidery I ever visited—anywhere in the country— was Citizen Cider. Whenever I came back to Burlington, I visited Citizen Cider, long before I'd begun this cider journey, even before Wassail had opened. Citizen Cider's tasting room was the first place I saw a dozen or more ciders on tap, the first place I tasted a 100 percent Northern Spy, and the first place I tasted a plum cider. Near a few of my favorite Burlington brew pubs, like Zero Gravity, I loved an easy-drinking Citizen Dry alongside a plate of poutine or during their Thursday night hot dog special. Citizen Cider made no secret about being a modern cidery, with a tanker truck parked out front in which they got deliveries of juice from local cider mills. Their ciders appealed to the growing hordes of beer enthusiasts in Vermont, and they fully embraced the craft beer vibe, with cool design, and ciders flavored with ginger (The Dirty Mayor), hops (Lakehopper), and "dry-ale style" cider called Wit's Up. They sold a bottled rosé cider called Brosé that was flavored with blueberries. Even my children love their non-alcoholic sparkling cider. But in my case, the deeper I dove into cider, the less Citizen's ciders appealed to me.

From a business standpoint, it's hard to argue with Citizen Cider's approach, which has resulted in explosive growth. They produced 5,000 gallons of cider when they launched in 2011. In 2017, they produced more than 450,000 gallons. The day after I visited Steve Wood at Farnum Hill, I met Cheray MacFarland, Citizen Cider's marketing director, at the tasting room. MacFarland had come from nearby Woodchuck Cider after it was sold to Irish cider company C&C Group for $305 million in 2012. "In a macro cider world, Citizen Cider is not on their scale," she said.

"Our approach is being the approachable cider," MacFarland told me, while I tasted Feral Fizz (a pet-nat cider with solid tannins), Sage Against the Machine (a weird, hibiscus-herbal thing), and Cori-Anderson (a gose-style cider). I also tried Wood, which is Citizen Cider's homage to Steve Wood of Farnum Hill.

There's a simple reason that Citizen Cider is always bringing out new styles and flavor. "Craft beer people are finicky and they're not loyal," MacFarland said. I wondered if the beer consumer is also the reason Citizen Cider sold mostly in kegs and cans. MacFarland said no, that canned cider is simply a reality of the marketplace. "Bottles are a dying breed. The bottle space on shelves is disappearing," she said. "It's strange. Because I always prefer bottles."

* * *

About 20 miles down the road, in the town of Vergennes, Shacksbury Cider straddles the line between modern and heritage approaches. Shacksbury Dry in a can (which they describe as "the lager of ciders") is now ubiquitous at places where cider is sold. At the same time, Shacksbury has, since the beginning, produced wild-foraged ciders for its Lost Apple Project. Limited-edition bottlings such as Deer Snacks (with 80 percent foraged apples) and Ticonderoga, aged in rye whiskey and Madeira barrels, have become coveted by cider geeks. They've done collaborations with numerous cideries, including an innovative transatlantic partnership with Petritegi in Spain's Basque region, which they import. They've also blended their juice with Petritegi's to create Arlo, possibly one of the most interesting canned ciders on the market. They've also collaborated with the beverage director at David Chang's restaurants to create a special Momofuku cider.

All of this has led to Shacksbury's impressive growth: They went from selling only 1,000 cases in 2014 to producing 40,000 gallons in 2016 and then 100,000 gallons in 2017. "We're not in this to be a mom-and-pop shop," said David Dolginow, who launched Shacksbury in 2013 with Colin Davis, with whom he graduated from nearby Middlebury College. When I met Dolginow and Davis at their new tasting room, which opened in late 2017, I drew a comparison to Citizen Cider and asked, "Will you ever get as big as them?"

"Hopefully much bigger," Davis said.

I drove with Davis to visit one of their partners, Sunrise Orchards, a large grower in Cornwall, in the Champlain Valley. In 2013, Dolginow had been working at Sunrise, funded by a grant, to find revenue streams of "value-added agriculture." Shacksbury grew out of this research.

The Shacksbury guys love to talk about their Lost Apple Project, which is a small portion of their business. "In a single day you can taste a thousand experiments that nature has conducted," said Davis, a Vermont native from nearby Shoreham. "But there's usually only one of each tree in existence." Like foragers in the Finger Lakes and the Hudson Valley, Shacksbury takes cuttings of scion wood from the wild seedlings they like and cultivates them. The big difference is scale. Shacksbury grafts its scion wood on a commercial scale in an orchard, with much bigger resources. "Foraging for apples is not a great way to run a business," Davis said. "So we went back to the trees that worked and took scion wood. We're bringing these wild apples into commercial production. Part of the project is about flavor and terroir. But the other part is about finding what grows in a commercial orchard." It's certainly a more sustainable business model than relying on a dying 160-year-old feral tree in the Catskills, like Andy Brennan does. Had the Shacksbury guys found that tree, that apple could have survived in their commercial orchard.

At Sunrise Orchards, we walked the rows of trees grafted from the wild seedlings. Some are now four or five years old, and will soon bear significant cider fruit. "This is Cutting Hill, because we found it on Cutting Hill Road," he said. "This is Galvin Russet. That's from Galvin Road. And this one is Animal Farm. It's from where they make Animal Farm Butter."

A few rows over, they have rows of Dabinett and Wickson Crab, which they got—naturally—from Steve Wood at Farnum Hill. Davis and Dolginow count Wood as one of their mentors. "I was sort of indoctrinated by Steve," Davis said, with a laugh. "But I'm starting to loosen up." Davis said he was excited to see that Farnum Hill had finally released a can. "I want Steve to be less dogmatic," he said.

When I returned to the Shacksbury tasting room a few week later, Dolginow was hosting a group of 15 students from the Middlebury College entrepreneurs club. He told the students about how wild apples were "really the core of our business," which played for big laughs. The ones that were 21 years old tasted some cider samples from the tanks. Dolginow told them, "What you're drinking now will eventually be a $25 cider that will be on the menu at restaurants in New York." He told them about the challenges: how the cider market is only $1 billion, compared to beer, which is $100 billon; how the trees they planted won't really bear productive fruit for half a decade; how they needed to work to "create compelling brand collaboration."

One of the students asked a question: "Was there ever a point where you were like, 'Am I going to fail? Is Shacksbury going to fail?'"

Dolginow thought about it for a second. "Nah, not really. We've had steady growth from the start."

The last piece of advice that Dolginow gave the Middlebury entrepreneur club: "You want to start a business with a million dollars. Starting with $200,000 is good. But a million is better."

CHAPTER 7

THE LOST ORCHARDS

A lot of people told me that Portland, Oregon, was a great cider town. So on my way out to Vancouver for my reporting on the Trump International Hotel & Tower, I stopped over. After a few days of drinking at the city's plethora of cider houses and cider bars, I would amend that slightly and call Portland—per the Style Guide of the United States Association of Cider Makers—a great *modern* cider town.

It was in Portland, and nowhere else, that I tasted ciders flavored with tamarind, lemongrass, and coriander. It was in Portland that I tasted a watermelon-ginger-lime cider by Reverend Nat's Hard Cider called Holy Water(melon), a tangerine-vanilla-sea-salt cider from Hi Five called Tangerine Submarine, and ciders from WildCraft Cider Works flavored with strawberry-spruce, peach-bourbon, and its Chesters Fresh Hop Bitterberry—with fresh hops and wild choke-berry bitters and chesterberries.

At Portland Cider Company (slogan "Always Hard"), I had a flight of ciders flavored variously with passion fruit, pumpkin spice, and honey, as well as their Pearfect Perry and Grape Storm (which seemed to be channeling a grape lollipop). At Schilling Cider House, I asked the server what the most popular cider was, and he told me, Grapefruit and Chill ("It's a take on Netflix and Chill," he explained). The next most popular cider, he said, was Chaider ("which is literally made with cider and chai"). Among the 50 ciders on tap were Schilling's own Pineapple Passion, Pom/Cran, and Rhubarb Pear along with nine hopped ciders, two pumpkin ciders, as well as raspberry, lingonberry, and marionberry ciders from various local producers.

It was striking that Portland's cider scene seemed based mostly on "semi-dry" or "off-dry" offerings that would taste sweet to many drinkers, especially those with a northeastern palate. Also, Portland cider fans apparently really love hops in their cider, as shown by one afternoon's "Fresh Hop micro-fest" in which I tasted Bauman's Fresh Hop, Finnriver Fresh Hop, Tieton Fresh Hop, Portland Cider Fresh Hop, Cider Riot Fresh Hop—as well as Schilling Fresh Hop Randall (with fresh hops and quince). The Finnriver Fresh Hop (made in Washington) happened to be delicious, but like so much of the cider I tasted in Portland, there was little discernible evidence of apples.

While there are certainly a handful of heritage (or "orchard-based") cideries in Oregon, Washington, and California, the West Coast seems to mostly be ground zero for modern, semi-dry cider. That's happened for a few reasons. Most obviously, the Pacific Northwest and California have a solid tradition of craft brewing innovation, and the cider from these regions has closely followed the craft beer model, with lots of snazzily designed cans, funny names, and crazy flavor combinations. What's also obvious is that local consumers in places like Portland and Seattle crave these types of modern and flavored ciders.

What's perhaps more complicated is West Coast cider makers' reliance on dessert fruit and juice concentrate—especially since Washington is the nation's largest apple-producing state (with California and Oregon both in the top 10). Likewise, California, Oregon, and Washington make up the majority of pear production. But so much of this fruit production comes from giant commercial orchards that focus on apple varieties such as Red Delicious, Golden Delicious, Granny Smith, Gala, and Pink Lady and pear varieties such as Bartlett and Bosc. Many of the less-common varieties in older orchards largely disappeared as the modern farm-to-supermarket system became standardized. Growers simply focused on what was easier to cultivate and sturdier to ship. Rising land prices also led to the sale of many smaller farms to developers, especially in places like Silicon Valley, which once was covered in orchards. There are fewer heirloom orchards here than in the Northeast.

So for whatever reason, most ciders from the West Coast would be categorized as modern because of the apples used. This means that, in the cider world, the divide between modern and heritage ciders is quickly becoming a West Coast—East Coast schism. As someone from the East Coast, who was educated in New England, I'm afraid I cannot be completely impartial.

* * *

After several days in Portland, I decided to drive south into the Willamette Valley, one of the country's great wine regions, famed for its pinot noir and pinot gris. In fact, the pinot gris in the Willamette Valley may be among the finest white wines made in America. I went to visit a cidery called Art + Science, whose stunning ciders I'd encountered at Wassail and other bars back East—made with foraged apples, pears, and even quince. Dry and tannic, Art + Science struck me as having an atypical point of view for the Pacific Northwest and felt similar to the cider revivalists I'd been spending my time with.

Before meeting the cider makers, I arrived in Willamina ("Timber Town USA") where I'd be staying. As cliché as this may sound: The Twin Peaks vibe was strong in Willamina. As I checked into the Wildwood Hotel, a group of people who identified themselves as a "team of paranormal investigators" was checking out, loading piles of equipment they had used in this investigation of the paranormal activity inside the hotel where I would be sleeping that night. "Did you find anything?" I asked one guy as he loaded his truck.

He smiled with wide eyes, and said, "Yup!" I looked at him to elaborate, and all he said was, "It was pretty cool!"

As I walked upstairs, a woman who was also part of the team pointed into one room and said, "Why don't you go look in the closet in there, where there's an old child's bed." I chose a different room.

A little while later, I met Kim Hamblin, who owns Art + Science with her husband, Dan Rinke. Hamblin, 46, likes to say that she's the "art" and she creates the distinctive labels with futuristic, glittery owls and swallows. She wore thick-rimmed glasses, her hair in two braids that hung from underneath a trucker hat that read WWOOF (the acronym for "World Wide Opportunities for Organic Farms").

I got into Hamblin's Honda hatchback (with license plate reading ARTSCI) and she drove me around the Willamette Valley, through the outskirts of farming communities such as Perrydale, Ballston, and Sheridan, where she forages her fruit. Since most of the large farms grow mass-market dessert fruit, Hamblin relies on finding fruit trees that hobbyists have planted or those grown in farmhouse yards as so-called "ornamentals." She knows most of the homes around here because she has a day job in real estate. "Though I've always been a reluctant real estate agent," she said.

We passed a farmhouse with a dozen apple trees in the yard. "I asked these people if I could have their apples, but they never got back to me. I should talk to them again," Hamblin said. "That's how I am. I just show up and am like 'hiiiii.' And they must be like, who is this crazy apple lady? People are happy for you to take their fruit. But sometimes they're a little paranoid to have you on their property." Along the road, we passed a tall tree with some crab apples hanging at the top. "I picked that tree as high as I could reach," she said. "That's the thing with foraging. Sometimes the trees are too tall." Another small orchard came up on our right, next to a trailer. "I stopped there once," she said. "I don't usually get sketched out, but these guys were sketching me out. I was like, 'These guys are going to kill me.' There was a real tweaker vibe."

Rows and rows of hazelnut trees line the roads here. "This is becoming Oregon's cash crop," she said. Hazelnuts? "Well, technically they're called filberts." Hamblin said that many organic farmers are worried about what the massive hazelnut agribusiness is doing to the region's soil.

About 25 minutes from Willamina, across from the Perrydale School, Hamblin pointed out a farmhouse with some quince trees in the yard. "I already picked those. I picked the snot out of those trees," she said. "I will go far and wide for quince. Most people don't use their quince." That's because, unlike with apples or pears, quince isn't eaten raw.

Down the road was another farm with a little orchard in the backyard. Hamblin pulled up, hopped out of the car, and gathered an armful of big yellow quince from off the ground. An older man came out to the porch. "Yuck," he said.

"They're beautiful!" Hamblin said.

"Not to me," he said. "We planted that tree for my brother-in-law. Me and the wife don't like them."

"The Wife" joined him on the porch. Hamblin greeted her and said, "Wow, the quince look great this year!"

"If you say so," said The Wife, eyeing her dubiously. She told Hamblin that she'd been waiting for her, but was getting impatient and about to post on Facebook about the quince so someone would come take them. "Will you take them today?" the woman asked.

"Well, I can be back in a day or two," Hamblin said.

"Well, OK. Tomorrow would be best."

The foraging dynamic is different with every single farm, Hamblin had told me earlier. "I don't necessarily tell them I run a cider business," she said. "I tell them if they ask, but if they don't, I don't say." As we drove, we passed a bunch of "TRUMP" and "Make American Great Again" signs. "There are some places I don't pick anymore because I really don't like the people," she said. "Also, some people around here are really religious and I can't always assume they'll be comfortable with alcoholic cider. I saw this one huge Gravenstein orchard, just dropping fruit. There must have been a hundred trees. But the people are super-duper religious." It reminded me that many Americans still believe, even today, that Prohibition seemed like a fine idea.

The old man with the quince tree was actually pretty nice and gave us a little tour of the other pear and apple trees, including some Gravenstein. The oldest he said had been planted in 1949. "After I put the chicken coop over there, it really grew." He wanted to cut down the quince tree. "It's getting in the way of my gardening," he said.

"No!" Hamblin said. "If you'll dig it up, I'll take it over to my place!"

After that, we drove another 10 minutes over to meet her husband, Dan Rinke (the "science" to Hamblin's "art"). Rinke, 42, works as a winemaker at Johan Vineyards, a biodynamic wine producer in nearby Rickreall known for its pinot noir, pinot gris, and grüner veltliner. Rinke is a tall, burly guy with a long, dark beard and on that day wore (wait for it) a flannel shirt.

Art + Science began when Rinke was looking for a raise, and since his employer didn't have the funds for that, Johan Vineyards agreed to let him use its facilities to create a side business. At first, he made some syrah and pinot noir for his own wine label, but when he and Kim bought their home farm in 2012, he realized that grapes wouldn't ripen there. "Plus, I was pretty frustrated with the wine industry at the time, so I was like, fuck it, let's do apples," he said. "Cider is wine. It's all the same thing." The first cider vintage was 2013. Apples quickly expanded to pears, quince, and other fruits. Rinke and Hamblin now make about 1,500 cases per year, all of it fermented with native yeast. Rinke and Hamblin were experimenting with blends of apples and wine grapes. We tasted a barrel of cider blended with grüner veltliner, with unique white pepper notes along with apple aromas, and another that was a blend of apples and sauvignon blanc, which had a pleasantly odd grapefruit note.

"I don't think a lot of people in the US know very much about cider," Rinke said. "Who, besides Farnum Hill, has more than ten vintages under their belt?"

After barrel tasting, Hamblin and Rinke drove 20 minutes over to what they called the Wilder Orchard. It's a private home with a neglected 20-year-old orchard on the property that the new owners, who'd moved in a couple months before, hoped to reclaim. They asked Hamblin and Rinke to help.

At the farmhouse, we were greeted by the homeowner, Mindy, gardening in her front yard. "Do you know when you're supposed to harvest olives?" she asked us. We all shrugged.

We walked the rows of unpruned and unhealthy apples trees, some suffering from fire blight and others simply in need of some love and care. "This is a rarity for the West Coast, to have an heirloom orchard like this," Rinke said.

"What varieties are these?" I ask.

"I have no idea," Rinke said. "I don't know varieties. I could tell you grapes all day long, but for apples I haven't even bothered ID'ing them. I'm blending everything, so what does it matter?"

When we got back into the car, Hamblin sighed and said, "I could see this getting cutthroat. I could see someone trying to get these apples from us." Hamblin talked about the inconsistency and uncertainty of foraging. She told a story about getting attacked by dogs at one orchard. Then there's the threatening farmer at one place whom she calls The Beltwhipper. That's because one day, as she was picking, this farmer saw her and angrily confronted her, took off his belt, and started snapping it in the air. "Ah, The Beltwhipper," she said. "But I keep going back because it's a great crab."

"We should take him to the meth heads," Rinke said.

"Yeah. They're totally sketchy," Hamblin said. "I started carrying pepper spray when I went to that orchard."

We pulled up to a dilapidated white farmhouse with a rusted roof and a few broken windows that looked abandoned. "We call this the Wooden Orchard," Hamblin said.

"Who owns this?" I asked.

Hamblin said, "This is owned by . . . well . . . technically . . . I don't know who really owns this. They keep saying they're saving the apples for this guy named Steven, who's sort of this Amish-like guy who rides horses and used to have a job breaking in Levi's for the Asian market. But Steven is never here." The 50 or so apple trees on this property were incredible, and full of hanging fruit. "I think the trees are from the 1940s, but I'm not sure." Hundreds of unpicked apples had already dropped onto the grass. Just like at the last orchard, the varieties were unknown. Hamblin jumped up and picked a russetted yellow apple, and said, "We call this one the Wooden Russet. We've taken cuttings to graft in our own orchard."

Later that evening, with snowy Mount Jefferson in the distance, Hamblin and Rinke took me on a tour of their farm, including their alpaca and sheep. Then we walked the five acres of apple trees they'd planted. Rinke grafted scion wood from various varieties that Hamblin had found, but there are also seedlings they've planted, including the indigenous *Malus fusca*, or Pacific crab apple. "We do not need a monoculture of the same eight cider varieties everyone is planting," Hamblin said.

Like a lot of cider makers who've planted an orchard in the past half decade, Hamblin and Rinke are still waiting for fruit. "I think we'll have a crop next year," Rinke said. "This year we had blossoms but the deer came in and ate them."

That night, over dinner, we tasted through their excellent Little Apples (made with foraged crab apples aged 10 months in wine barrels), Wild Perry, and various ciders with quince. The 100 percent quince was really wild, untamed, and tannic, but blended with apples, it was one of the most otherworldly ciders I've tasted. It was a million miles away from a cider flavored with tangerine-vanilla-sea-salt or watermelon-ginger-lime.

As we moved on to Mountain Rose, made with a green-skinned, pink-fleshed apple, I told them I was a little scared to go back to my haunted hotel. Hamblin and Rinke did not help matters when they told me that the hotel had once been a brothel and everyone knew about the ghost of a prostitute who'd died there. "But the owner told me the paranormal team had only found nonthreatening ghosts," Hamblin said. "Apparently one asked the investigators to dance with her." This did not exactly calm my fears. I did not sleep well that night, though it might have been more from the noise of timber trucks rumbling through downtown Willamina all night long.

In the morning, I ate a chicken-fried steak and eggs at Coyote Joe's and then met Hamblin at the farmhouse of the older couple we'd met the day before, to pick their quince tree. "This tree looks like a candidate for a shake," she said when I arrived. She climbed up amid the quince and started violently shaking the branches, as huge hard quince fell to the ground. "Watch your head," she said. "A quince hitting you in the head isn't going to feel good." In all, we gathered about six bushels, which would make approximately two to three gallons of cider. Hamblin made sure to clip some branches so they could graft this tree and cultivate it in their orchard.

"It's amazing how many people plant fruit trees for no good reason," she said.

"Do you think it's just for the blossoms in springtime?" I asked.

"Yeah, people like the blossoms," she said. "But also I think people just like the idea of planting fruit trees."

About six months later, Hamblin sent me ciders from the places we'd visited. Sadly, she told me that the old man had finally chopped down the quince tree we'd picked that day.

* * *

Six hundred miles south of the Willamette Valley is another famous wine region: Sonoma County, California. Sonoma is the home of Tilted Shed Ciderworks, one of a handful of producers in California working organically with heirlooms, bittersharps, and bittersweets. California has nearly as many cideries as New York, but most of them are making modern ciders.

Ellen Cavalli, who owns Tilted Shed with her husband, Scott Heath, is also the publisher of the zine *Malus*, which has become a sort of serial, staple-folded manifesto for the heritage cider world, or as Cavalli calls it, "an op-ed page that merged with a chapbook that crashed into an antiquarian print shop." Besides zine publishing, Cavalli and Heath are also excellent cider makers. Tilted Shed's Graviva, made from 50 percent Gravenstein and a blend of Rome, Nehou, and Muscat de Bernay is a wonderfully complex example of what California cider can be. Its Lost Orchard bottling, from feral apples picked in an abandoned orchard in western Sonoma County, rivals the sorts of wild-foraged ciders made in New York and New England.

I had seen Cavalli at Cider Days in Massachusetts, and she told me about a collaboration cider she'd recently done with apples from a historic orchard at Filoli, the beautifully preserved early-20th-century estate and gardens in Woodside, California, that is overseen by the National Trust for Historic Preservation. Filoli delivered 80 varieties of apples to Tilted Shed, who made a cider for sale in the estate's gift shop.

Filoli's 10-acre "gentleman's orchard" contains some 600 fruit trees, about 115 of which date back to 1918, when the original owner, prominent San Francisco entrepreneur William Bowers Bourn II, planted them. I'd been to Filoli and a number of other historic orchards in California a couple of years before for a feature I wrote for *Preservation* magazine. "This orchard allows us to educate people on the story of fruit before the mid-20th century, before we had easy access to fruit like we do today," said Jim Salyards, Filoli's head of horticulture. "There are definitely varieties in here that we haven't identified yet." Filoli had been donated to the National Trust in 1975, and the orchard stood mostly untouched for about two decades, until preservation began in earnest in the 1990s.

I gathered with a group of gardeners to tour the orchard, which boasts 277 varieties of apples, 59 varieties of pears, and dozens of even rarer specimens of other pome and stone fruit. Cavalli told me that the place had been "heaven" for her and I, too, could barely contain my excitement. All around me, brilliant fruit popped from the trees in reds, yellows, greens. Tiny signs next to each tree listed names of fruit I'd yet to hear about in my travels: apples named Lords Seedling, Claygate Pearmain, Court Pendu Gris, Reinette Marbrée, Hudson's Golden Gem, Laxton's Superb, Horneburger Pfannkuchen, and Duchess of Oldenburg; pears named Moonglow, Jargonelle, and Clapp's Favorite.

Our guide, Carolyn Curtis, was a volunteer docent who usually led orchard tours for the public. This, however, was a special training tour for members of Filoli's professional horticulture staff, and I was allowed to tag along. As our group wandered into the orchard, Curtis pointed out a Wolf River apple. "This ripens in August and it's enormous," she said. "The only reason people ever grew it was to win first prize at the county fair for biggest apple." In the next row, Curtis grabbed a bright yellow apple. "This is called a Winter Banana," she said. "It's a wonderful heirloom variety. It was planted pre-1975, though we don't know when."

Someone asked if we could taste it. Salyards pulled out a knife and cut a few slices to pass around. "Usually, this is not a U-Pick sort of place," Curtis said, with a chuckle. "We discourage the public from picking fruit. People show up for tours with shopping bags, but that's not what we do here." It suddenly felt like we were biting into Forbidden Fruit.

"It's true," said Salyards. "We're trying to preserve the original landscape. It's more about keeping the trees alive. The fruit is just a bonus." But Salyards couldn't help but share that bonus. He grabbed a Kasseler Reinette, the size of a tennis ball, from another tree and sliced it. As we shared the apple, our group agreed that it was the tastiest one yet, crisp and bracingly tart, but with a pleasantly sweet lingering finish.

We watched a heron take off from an apple tree, along with bluebirds, butterflies, and even a pack of wild turkeys. A local beekeeper's hive stood in a corner near black walnut trees. Salyards pointed out gaps in rows where pear trees had been lost. "We've had some really tough years with drought and disease," he said. Fire blight has hit the orchard particularly hard in years past.

Curtis led us to a San Juan Battista Mission pear tree, which dates to the 1820s. "These aren't gourmet pears," she said. "But you keep this tree because it's a link to the padres," the Spanish missionaries who settled in California. Salyards grabbed a Kieffer pear from a nearby tree. Afterward, he plucked a couple of fresh figs, then two different types of persimmon, and then a rare hawthorn fruit. We shared tiny bits of each.

By now, our rare-fruit tasting was clearly making Curtis a bit uncomfortable. "This is more tasting than we would normally do," she said. The public generally only gets one chance each year to taste the orchard's fruit, at the annual Autumn at Filoli Festival. Two to three tons are also donated annually to a local food bank.

But Salyards and his staff can be forgiven for their enthusiasm. After all, they are the ones who prune in January, fight disease and pests, thin the fruit in the spring, trap and relocate varmints such as gophers and deer, and harvest the fruit over eight weeks in late summer and fall. "Orchards are a ton of work. You can spend endless time in there," Salyards said. "When orchards are in fruit they're very exciting. But for the rest of the year, they're not as sexy as flowers or the rest of the gardens."

After that, we wandered among the peach trees and the black walnut trees. Finally, we came upon a very odd tree that Curtis identified as medlar—the mythical pome fruit that pops up in literary works ranging from Cervantes' *Don Quixote* to Shakespeare's *Romeo and Juliet*. To Curtis' relief, we couldn't eat anything from this tree, because medlar needs to be ripened, softened, and bletted, not consumed raw. Several members of the group, myself in particular, were crestfallen.

Still, Curtis told us about the flavor of this historic fruit with unbridled glee. "The taste is unlike anything else," she said. "The closest I can say is that it tastes like apple sauce with cinnamon. And some people say it tastes like a fruitcake." Curtis smiled at us, and then gave us perhaps the best reason of all for preserving orchards. "You just don't taste a flavor like this," she said. "Unless you grow it."

* * *

California, with its rich fruit-growing history, is at the forefront of orchard preservation. About a decade ago, the California Department of Parks and Recreation created a Historic Orchard Assessment program. Surveys showed that at least 44 of its state parks had potential historic orchards, and the state now offers expert advice, training, treatment, and management for them. That means there's the potential for many cider projects like the one Tilted Shed and Filoli have collaborated on. Perhaps even Big Cider could work with some of these historic orchards.

For instance, at Fort Ross State Historic Park in Jenner, California, a handful of fruit trees date back to the 1820s, when the fort was occupied by the original Russian settlers. "Those trees are the only truly, 100 percent Russian artifacts," said Susan Rudy, the orchard specialist at Fort Ross. "The buildings have been renovated or moved. But up in the orchard, the trees are still there." Fort Ross has three capulin cherry trees that the Russian settlers acquired from the Santa Cruz Mission in the 1820s. "They flower and fruit every year. When trees have been hanging around that long, they tend to have some tenacity," Rudy said. "They're a living resource. But that's also a frightening idea, because they have an end date." Just like people, they ultimately have a life span.

Historic orchards give us not only a sense of how people farmed, worked, and lived in the past, they also represent a record of the sorts of tastes historically enjoyed. Because fruit has always provided humans with natural access to sweetness—as well as alcohol through fermentation—we may even get a sense of a former era's small pleasures. "Sugar was super expensive. So if you wanted something sweet, you had to be growing and preserving fruit to add some excitement to your diet," said Salyards.

At the center of sprawling San Jose, in the city's Guadalupe River Park and Gardens, lives a 3.3-acre orchard with 200 fruit trees. This historic orchard commemorates what the Santa Clara Valley was before the tech industry took over and it became known as Silicon Valley. Leslee Hamilton, Guadalupe River Park's executive director, could remember growing up amid miles of fruit blossoms in the South Bay. She recalled sneaking into neighbors' orchards to eat apricots and then, when she was older, working at a local canning company, "cutting 'cots" in the summertime. "The rise of high-tech put pressure on land values," Hamilton said. "This is a living laboratory. This is about preserving fruit varieties that put Santa Clara Valley on the map." Among the fruit produced by the orchard's trees are Blenheim and Moore Park apricots, Silver Logan peaches, Italian plums, cherries, pomegranates, and elderberries.

But Hamilton admitted that Guadalupe River Park's historic orchard faced a number of stresses. The park and orchard are bordered by the busy San Jose Market Center, filled with big-box retailers such as Target, Office Depot, and PetSmart. Hamilton says some in the city have suggested that the best use of the park and orchard would be bulldozing it and putting in a parking lot. Beyond that, California's recent five-year drought hurt the trees. Packs of squirrels treat them like a fruit buffet. And even though posted city signs prohibit removing fruit from the orchard without permission, there is still a good deal of theft. Last year, when volunteers showed up to harvest the cherry trees and donate the fruit to a local food bank, they found that the entire crop had been picked clean, stolen. "It's maddening," said Hamilton. "The city hasn't had a whole lot of resources to help."

Before I left San Jose, I drove over to J&P Farms, another orchard and farm market tucked away in a suburban neighborhood among contemporary-style homes. "Welcome to the last orchard in San Jose," read the chalkboard. "Help yourself and please put money in the slot." Boxes hold Casselman plums, fresh figs and dates, Muscat of Alexandria grapes—and, according to the handwritten sign: "Best Apples You Ever Ate." An older man busied himself behind the counter. I chatted with him, and confirmed that this is indeed the last commercial orchard in San Jose. "It's sad," he said. "San Jose used to be the fruit capital of the world."

A few hours north of San Jose, and even more off-the-beaten path, is a 26-acre, nearly 100-year-old orchard that was acquired by Jack London State Historic Park, in the Sonoma County village of Glen Ellen. As Eric Metz, director of operations for the park, and Breck Parkman, senior archaeologist with the state's Department of Parks and Recreation, drove me up to the orchard on a winding mountain road, we passed a sign that warns visitors about mountain lions. I raised my eyebrow, and Parkman said, "Yep, we have mountain lions. And lots of rattlesnakes, too."

At about 1,000 feet above sea level, we got out of the truck and trekked into the orchard. It was difficult, at first, to discern the overgrown apple, quince, plum, and apricot trees from the rest of the wild area. "Look at all that coyote scat," Parkman said. "The coyote definitely eat the fruit." Then he points out a wood rats' nest. "For wood rats, this orchard is a gourmet delicatessen," he said. That's part of the challenge in preserving the area, he continued. "I may see a historic orchard here. But our naturalist sees a wildlife habitat." Here was the opposite of Michael Pollan's assertion in *The Botany of Desire* that an orchard was idealized, domesticated proof that settlers had "mastered the primordial forest." Here, the forest had reclaimed the human creation.

The orchard's heyday had been in the 1930s and 1940s, when it was operated by what is now called the Sonoma Developmental Center, a historic facility for people with developmental disabilities. In those days, family members sent children to live here full-time. The center ran a cannery, and records from 1953 show they sold

15,000 pounds of apples that year. But by the 1960s, the cannery and orchard had ceased operation. "This orchard was untouched for decades," said Metz. "It's becoming a natural state."

In 2007, after a few years of study, the national and state park services issued an orchard assessment and the arduous work of reclaiming and restoring the orchard began in earnest. But funding has been a challenge. Facing severe budget cuts in 2012, the state nearly closed Jack London State Historic Park, which would have meant the demise of the orchard. "Orchards are living things. They require a lot of care," Parkman said.

In the future, Metz hopes to replant using cuttings and rootstock from the remaining historic trees, to preserve the genetic stock. "We're trying to protect the cultural and historic landscape," he said. "But every acre we clear is an acre we have to maintain."

When Tilted Shed's Cavalli and I corresponded about her cider project at Filoli, I told her about this wild mountain orchard—just like I tell every cider revivalist with an interest in old orchards. I hope someday to see a cider from this fruit for sale in the gift shop of Jack London State Historic Park.

* * *

When I returned home from the West Coast, I had to immediately leave again, this time for Virginia.

Just like Oregon's Willamette Valley or New York's Finger Lakes, Virginia's Albemarle County is both wine *and* cider country. People often forget about Virginia as one of the great cider regions in the nation, and there are a number of very good cideries in this county that surrounds Charlottesville, such as Castle Hill Cider, Potter's Craft Cider, and Albemarle CiderWorks. Thomas Jefferson, unsurprisingly, grew cider apples at nearby Monticello, including Esopus

Spitzenburg, Hewe's Virginia Crab, and Newtown Pippin—which around here is called Albemarle Pippin. Jefferson's most beloved apple was the Taliaferro (or "Tolliver"), which he called "the best cyder apple existing," and produced "unquestionably the finest cyder we have ever known, and more like wine than any other liquor I have ever tasted which was not wine." Sadly, the Taliaferro is now extinct. There aren't even any illustrations of the Taliaferro, and its only description comes from a pomologist in 1835, who wrote: "The fruit is the size of a grape shot, or from one to two inches in diameter; of a white color, streaked with red; with a sprightly acid, not good for the table, but apparently a very valuable cider fruit." Still, apple geeks throughout the country hold out hope that they may someday rediscover the apple. As Peter Hatch, Monticello's director emeritus of gardens and grounds once wrote, "the enigma of the lost Taliaferro has elevated its stature among historic apple hunters to almost mythic qualities, and handfuls of potential candidates . . . reappear like migratory birds every season." Yet Hatch concluded that "Jefferson's mystery apple will never be found."

Another, more recent, president also owns some property in Albemarle County down the road from Monticello. "I own, actually, one of the largest wineries in the United States. It's in Charlottesville," boasted President Trump after a press conference at Trump Tower in August 2017. This was the press conference in which he addressed the clash between white supremacists and those protesting a statue of Robert E. Lee that resulted in a neo-Nazi killing a woman with his car. There were "very fine people on both sides," Trump had said. Perhaps unsurprisingly, Trump does not in fact own the largest winery in the country. Not even close. But Trump does indeed own a bustling winery in Albemarle County, in the heart of Virginia's wine country. And I ended up there because of my endless *Washington Post Magazine* assignment.

Several months after the ugly skirmish in Charlottesville, I stood at the bar of the Trump Winery tasting room, just 14 minutes down the road from Monticello and a half mile up Blenheim Road from Dave Matthews' Blenheim Vineyards. It was a sunny autumn Sunday, and the tasting room was packed, with a security guard scanning the crowd. A young woman shoved her way in next to me, and said, "Can I just get a taste of the chardonnay?" Behind me, at a table, a man spilled an entire bottle of red wine down the front of him, and a woman spritzed him off with a water bottle. "Can I taste the sparkling rosé?" the young woman next to me asked. No, she was told. She had to be a member of the Trump Wine Club to taste the sparkling rosé. I paid $15 for a tasting of five wines. The sparkling Blanc de Blancs and the mildly oaked chardonnay were passable; the "meritage" Bordeaux blend and the cabernet sauvignon were fruit bombs and sort of meh; and the CRU dessert wine that's aged in Jack Daniel's barrels was a sweet-toothache disaster.

After the Trump wine tasting, I decided to move from wine to cider. I drove 20 minutes up the road to Albemarle CiderWorks in North Garden. There, I tasted a dry, single-varietal bottling of Albemarle Pippin. I also had beautiful ciders made from three apple varieties you don't often see in the North: Black Twig, Arkansas Black, and Harrison. Black Twig is the official state apple of Tennessee and was the favorite of Andrew Jackson. Arkansas Black is exactly as it sounds, a dark, blackish-red apple that was first found in the Ozarks in the 1820s. Tom Burford, a respected nurseryman, fruit historian, and author of the classic book *Apples of North America*, writes: "As a boy, my father warned me never to hit anyone in the head with this very hard apple: it would kill." Albemarle CiderWorks' single-varietal Arkansas Black, with big tannins and a note of birch-beer-like bitterness, was truly exceptional.

But it was the cider made from Harrison that fascinated me most. The Harrison apple first appeared in early 19th-century New Jersey and the prized cider made from it was once called "Newark Champagne." The noted pomologist William Coxe wrote, in 1817, of Harrison's "high coloured, rich, and sweet cider of great strength, commanding a high price in New York, frequently ten dollars and upwards per barrel when fined for bottling." But by the mid-20th century—just like Jefferson's Taliaferro—Harrison had disappeared, thought to be extinct. Then, in 1976, an orchardist named Paul Gidez used Coxe's 19th-century description to track down a single Harrison tree at an old cider mill in Livingston, New Jersey. Burford, the author and fruit historian, helped verify its identity. In a 2010 interview with *Edible Jersey* magazine, Burford called Harrison "the most enigmatic apple I've ever dealt with. When I first tasted it I had to sit down. I was so unsettled. How could it have happened that this great cider apple got pushed out of production?" Harrison is now grown mostly in Virginia, though there has been some effort to revive it in the Garden State.

During my visit to Albemarle CiderWorks, I saw boxes full of Harrison, Black Twig, and Arkansas Black, plus other heirlooms like York, Razor Russet, and Grimes Golden, all for sale outside the tasting room. Customers kept popping inside to pay for bags of apples. As I tasted, I chatted with Charlotte Shelton, one of three Shelton siblings in the cidery and orchard. I'd met her brother Chuck at Cider Days in Massachusetts, where the Albemarle Pippin had been poured by Dan Pucci and Darlene Hayes along with other Newtown Pippin ciders from around the world.

Shelton told me that Albemarle wants to focus on American heirloom varieties. "Everyone is trying to grow English varieties like Kingston Black, Dabinett," she said. "We should not be producing

English cider or Spanish cider. We want to make American cider." She also pushed back on the notion that only heirlooms, bitter-sharps, and bittersweets made good cider. "That's balderdash," she said. "There are a lot of wretched heirloom apples. And there are plenty of great-tasting modern apples." In any case, those types of apples could never meet demand. "There aren't enough cider apples in America if you're going to do a mass-produced cider," she said.

One fascinating blend at Albemarle CiderWorks was its Jupiter's Legacy, made from a blend of 20 varieties, including crab apples. The name comes from Jupiter Evans, who had been Thomas Jefferson's personal slave for more than 50 years. Jupiter was the only one Jefferson trusted to make cider at Monticello. "Jefferson said in his papers that the cider was never as good after Jupiter died," Shelton said.

* * *

After tasting cider, I drove up to the Albemarle Estate, the 26,000-square-foot, 45-room manor house that Trump converted into a luxury boutique hotel. It is gated and a sign reads that entrance is for registered guests only, "no tours." Since I had booked a room, the gate opened, and I drove a good three or four minutes up a rolling hill, past a croquet lawn and a chapel, before I arrived at the manor. Albemarle Estate has a decidedly less romantic story than Monticello. It was built in the 1980s by late billionaire John Kluge (at one time the richest man in America) and his then-third wife Patricia Kluge, who also owned the winery. After their divorce and John Kluge's death, Patricia had fallen on hard times, defaulted on loans, and by 2012 was facing foreclosure. That's when Trump swooped in to buy the estate at a fire-sale price.

The guest rooms are all named after Virginia presidents, and I stayed in Monroe. There's also Washington, Jefferson, Madison, and even, on the second floor, a Harrison room—our short-lived "log cabin and hard cider" president. My room here was even more over-the-top than at the other Trump properties: an ornate gold-trimmed bed with a crown-like headboard; shelves with knick-knacks like pewter goblets; golden faucets and gold accents, like a gold soap dish, glisten throughout the bathroom. And the branding, even for a Trump property, bordered on absurd. Here, besides the robe, the slippers, and the toiletries, I got TRUMP mouthwash and a TRUMP hair comb. On the desk was the pièce de résistance: the huge, lavishly illustrated *TRUMP Magazine*, with breathless travel features on the Trump golf courses, a photo-essay on "A Day in the Life of a Trump Bride," and a piece on the Trump Cookie at his golf club in Bedminster, New Jersey.

At 6 P.M. was a tour of the estate grounds, given by the hotel manager; I gathered with a half dozen other guests. The tour mixed practicalities with what I guess we might loosely call the "historical." Since the Albemarle Estate only dates back to the 1980s, and only has had one owner before Trump, the big themes espoused by the guide appeared to be: a) how crazily spendthrift the Kluges were, and how that led to their financial ruin; b) what a cunning and opportunistic businessman Donald Trump was for buying this $100 million mansion for only $6.2 million. Another big theme of the tour seemed to be how the Trumps have better taste than the Kluges. We walked through hallways plastered with gaudy wallpaper that looked like a Roman toga hanging on a curtain rod, and we looked out the big windows at the faux-classical sculptures and faux-English hedges and fountains in a garden that looked as though they were dreamed up by a mafia don pretending to be a British aristocrat. We wandered down a grand hallway that looked like a Jersey McMansion version of Versailles imagined by Donatella Versace, and our guide showed us garish busts of Jefferson and Washington. In the theater, we saw framed photos of Trump with celebrities like Sylvester Stallone, Christian Bale, and Kirk Douglas, as well as Trump on the covers of *Billionaire* magazine and the Forbes 400 "Richest People in America" issue from 2003.

The tour ended at the pool house. "There's a restroom right around the corner and there's a bunch of pool towels in the closet," said our guide. "Basically, this is y'all's house while you're here." That may be because the Albemarle Estate was run on a skeleton staff, and we were sort of on our own. A shift change came in a few hours, when the place would be staffed by a lone employee. There was no kitchen, so I went to Charlottesville for dinner. Later, when I returned, only the night manager was stirring. He offered me a jar of stale cookies to eat, the only snack available at that hour. In the library and billiards room, I grabbed a cue from under a bust of Julius Caesar and shot some pool on the big red table while I watched a football game on television. I was surrounded by shelves full of random books that seemed to have been curated by a decorator who'd said, "Just go get me some books, any books!" But there was one prominent shelf with Trump's own titles, including *The Best Real Estate Advice I Ever Received* and *The Way to the Top: The Best Business Advice I Ever Received*.

Instead of drinking Trump wine, I decided to open one of the ciders I'd bought at Albemarle CiderWorks, the one made from 100 percent Albemarle—or Newtown—Pippin. I sipped the cider made from one of the same apples that Jefferson's slave, Jupiter Evans, had used at Monticello. As I did, I wondered what happened to the elusive Taliaferro apple. Was that variety's disappearance the reason that the cider at Monticello was "never as good" once Jupiter died? This was leading to deeper, darker thoughts about heritage and American presidents. The Albemarle Pippin cider was crisp and lovely. But it didn't pair very well with the stale cookies.

CHAPTER 8
TXOTX, Y'ALL!

When you think of cider, you probably don't immediately think of the nation's capital. In fact, less than a decade ago, when I would write articles for the *Washington Post* about cider, they'd be met with a deafening silence and indifference. Now, however, one of the most innovative cider makers in the United States happens to be an urban cidery in the District of Columbia, called Anxo (pronounced *an-CHO*).

Anxo is a common first name in Spain's Basque region, as well as a nickname for Basajaun, a mythological creature that is sort of like a benevolent Basque Bigfoot. Basajaun, as the legend goes, taught humans agriculture, ironworking, and shepherding, then retreated to the darkness of the forest where he remains a bridge between the natural world and humanity. Similarly, Anxo Cidery, which also operates two tapas bars in the District, offers a bridge between the two wildly different worlds of Spanish and American cider, as well as between heritage and modern ciders. With his long red beard and shaggy hair, Sam Fitz, Anxo's gregarious, knowledgeable co-owner, may also be channeling the hairy mythical Basque creature.

Fitz came to cider from the world of craft beer—he was the first certified Cicerone in DC. But in 2014, Fitz made a trip to Spain's Basque Country and tasted Basque cider for the first time. To say that the experience was transformative is an understatement. "I grew up without any connection to apples," he said. "Then I went to Spain. And I realized the cider world had something that the beer world can just never have. What I was drinking was a connection of modern life and I guess a sort of old way of life." After that epiphany in Spain, Fitz left craft beer behind for cider.

Anxo launched and opened its original bar in the summer of 2016, just northeast of the hip Shaw neighborhood, and it was an immediate success. Anxo had a new sort of vibe, a place where groups of newbies could casually experience real, traditional cider, served with Spanish dishes like tortilla, pulpo, chorizo, pan con tomate, and anchovies. Servers dramatically hold bottles high over their heads to do long Spanish-style pours. There is cider education, but often it comes from the spout of a traditional Spanish porrón, passed around the table, until maybe one tipsy friend finally spills it all over himself. "Cider should not only appeal to a small group of people," Fitz said. "There's not just one cider consumer."

The following summer, Anxo opened a tasting room at its cidery location, at the northern border of the District. In the first year, they produced more than 20,000 gallons of cider. That summer, Anxo hired a full-time cider maker, Greg Johnson, who had worked at Virtue Cider with Ryan Burk before Burk moved on to Angry Orchard and Virtue was acquired by Anheuser-Busch InBev. At its launch, Anxo relied on making collaboration ciders, particularly in partnership with producers such as Farnum Hill, Shacksbury, and Eden. But as they've grown, their own style has evolved.

I toured the cidery with Fitz and Johnson just a few months after it opened in fall 2017. Above the bar, they were still constructing the barrel room, and they'd just acquired three huge Italian wine barrels, as well as several traditional sherry butts from Jerez, Spain. Johnson made his philosophy clear: "I don't want to make a hopped cider, a spiced cider, a raspberry cider." He told me that when he first moved to Washington from the Midwest, he'd visited the National Arboretum, and noticed a number of amazing apple trees. He was dying to forage there. "We're so young," he said. "This is our first real season."

Anxo's flagship is Cidre Blanc, made from 100 percent Gold Rush—the same dessert apples that Kite & String in the Finger Lakes was also excited about—fermented with sauvignon blanc yeast, and unfiltered. It's a fascinating hybrid: a cider with modern, mass-market potential that's made with a heritage approach. They also have a great series of ciders called Happy Trees—a reference to Bob Ross, host of the beloved PBS instructional art show, *The Joy of Painting*. My favorite Happy Trees is wild-fermented and made entirely with Arkansas Black apples grown in Virginia. Fitz and Johnson also make great ciders from Harrison, the prized New Jersey apple once thought to be extinct.

But the spiritual core of Anxo's offerings is its Sidra Verde, aged in a Basque cider barrel, and channeling a traditional Basque cider, wild fermented and unfiltered, with pronounced tartness, and pleasant but volatile acidity. Anxo's decision to embrace the Spanish cider tradition rather than that of England or France, or the early American traditions from New England and New York, feels inspired to me.

That's likely because I already happen to love high-acid, funky wines and beers. I also happen to love Spanish cider, and advocated for it a number of times in the *Washington Post* in the late 2000s. I've traveled to Spain fairly often for drinks reporting, and my first experiences were with Asturian cider, not Basque. One of my favorite side trips was in 2009, when I drove several hours north from the Castilla y León wine regions to Asturias, ascending into the mountains, cruising through long tunnels, watching the whole landscape and climate change. Where Castilla y León had been arid, hot, and sunny, Asturias was verdant green, cool, and overcast. Asturias is not the Spain of flamenco and bullfights. Here, there's a Celtic heritage that predates the Romans.

Asturias is all about *sidra*. Asturians drink about 100 liters of their beloved cider each year. "You will never see a region anywhere else where people drink so much cider," said Jose Luis Roza, then the commercial director at Trabanco, the cider producer I visited near the city of Gijón. "The Spanish economy is terrible, but the cider houses in Asturias are full."

Gijón is a bustling port city, and the ancient Cimedevilla neighborhood is full of wonderful old maritime atmosphere, especially at night when the *sidrerías* begin to fill up. Here, you order sidra by the liter bottle. "You cannot order a glass of cider," Roza said. With tremendous dexterity, bartenders or waiters will pour out the cider in a long stream, holding the bottle high over their heads and splashing a little bit down into a glass held at waist level—*escanciar la sidra*—so as to release the carbonic gas. You are served a couple of fingers of the agitated, cloudy cider, which you are then expected to drink in one gulp. You don't want to let it go flat.

Sidra drinking is serious session drinking, and I was blown away by the staggering amount of cider that the people in Gijón consume. For instance, at Sidrería Principado—where I paired my cider with amazing sardines drizzled with balsamic vinegar—I stood next to a middle-aged couple who casually tossed back three liters in about a half hour. "Asturians are Celtic, similar to the Irish. But when it comes to drinking, we consider the Irish juniors," Roza said.

So while you can find brands such as Trabanco in the United States if you look hard enough, why don't we see more Asturian cider in the United States? One reason is that more than 90 percent is consumed in Asturias. In fact, until a decade ago, most brands didn't even put a label on the bottle. Secondly, because Asturian and Basque ciders are not carbonated, you need someone with the skills to do the long-range cider pour, which creates natural effervescence. "The problem for Trabanco, of course, is that in the US, in a typical city, you will not find a waiter who can pour like this," Roza said.

This was before cideries like Anxo appeared on the scene.

* * *

I met Sam Fitz again at my first Franklin County Cider Days, where he sat on a panel called "Making Spanish-Style Cider (Sidra) in America" inside the white clapboard community center in historic Deerfield, Massachusetts. "Spanish cider has taken off in the American imagination in a way that other European ciders have not," Fitz told the audience. "But we struggled for over a year before we opened about how we should present sidra."

The rise of Spanish-style ciders, like most new tastes, is not without controversy and debate. Many cider people don't appreciate *sidra natural*'s lack of carbonation and the element of acetic acid. When inert, this acetic acid can seem vinegar-like and some—wrongly, in my opinion—consider it a flaw. This reaction against Spanish-style ciders seems to come from places where sweeter ciders are more popular. For instance, one Portland, Oregon, cider maker, told NPR in a 2017 interview: "We say, 'Oh yeah, this cider went bad, so we just put it into green bottles and called it Spanish.'" Many within the cider industry have unfortunately taken to classifying Spanish-style ciders as "sour"—likening them to sour beers.

In the same NPR piece, Ellen Cavalli, co-owner of Tilted Shed Ciderworks in Sonoma, California, who makes a sidra-inspired bottling called Inclinado, said it was "reductive" to call Spanish ciders sour. "These ciders are so much more complex than that," Cavalli said. "But if the word *sour* is going to push the category forward in the US, then I'll go with it."

On the Cider Days panel, Fitz appeared alongside Cavalli's husband, Scott Heath, as well as Ryan Burk from Angry Orchard, and Brian Rutzen, a cider buyer for The Northman, a cider bar in Chicago. Also present was John Reynolds, the troublemaker from Blackduck in the Finger Lakes, who makes the Spanish-style *¡No Pasarán!*

in which he allows the pomace to macerate for significant time, as they do in Asturias.

"What makes a sidra a sidra?" was the question posed to the panel. The idea of defining sidra as "sour" came up almost immediately. Rutzen insisted that "sour-forward ciders" were helping cider "gain legitimacy among craft beer people."

Reynolds called it "semantics," and said, "I don't think we have a say in the matter. They're going to call it 'sour.' That's how they're going to appeal to the beer drinkers. To me it's a beer thing, tied to the hype of sour beers. If that lures people over to cider, do we really care?"

Burk heatedly disagreed. "The term *sour*, in my view, is harmful," he said. "Sour is a disservice to the category. The Spanish don't talk about sour. Only Americans do." Burk also produces an Asturian-inspired cider at Angry Orchard, called Edu—which I'd tasted at the Innovation Cider House in Walden. His connection with the Spanish cider industry is why Angry Orchard paid for a group of rival New York cider makers to tour Asturias and Basque Country, so they could experience the traditional cider culture.

As the panel debated, volunteers came around the room with the various ciders from Spain and the US for us to sample. They gamely attempted to do the long Spanish pour, some of it managing to splash into our glasses. Another volunteer trailed behind them with a mop to clean up all the spilled cider.

Rutzen said the long pour was an important part of the appeal. "It's messy, it's funny," he said. "There's something about the ritual and the visual that people want to be part of."

As cider continued to spill onto the floor of the Deerfield Community Center, Reynolds said, "Nowhere has a culture around cider like Spain. It probably takes a 40-year dictatorship of a fascist to maintain a culture like that. So maybe sidra will take off 35 years from now in the US?"

* * *

A couple of months after that afternoon at Cider Days, after the holidays had passed, I made my own pilgrimage to experience the cider culture in the Basque region, the same one that had caused Fitz's cider epiphany.

No one really tells you what to do when you first arrive at a *sagardotegi*, or traditional Basque cider house, especially if you don't speak Basque. You're simply given a glass, led to one of the long wooden tables in a vast room, and immediately served a plate of chorizo, followed by a cod omelet. It's left up to you to figure out how to get a drink.

My brother Tyler and I learned this on our first night in Astigarraga, minutes southeast of San Sebastián, which happens to be the cider capital of Spanish Basque Country. In this town of just under 6,000 people, there are an astonishing 19 cider houses. We spent several days here in late January, at the start of the traditional cider season that runs through April. With Spanish-style ciders becoming more popular among American cider makers and cider enthusiasts, I wanted to see what they tasted like at the source.

At Gartziategi, a sagardotegi in a big stone barn on the outskirts of town, we learned that when a guy with a bucket yells "txotx!" (pronounced "choach") it means he's about to open the tap on one of dozens of huge 13,000-liter barrels, shooting out a thin stream of cider. You're supposed to stand up from your meal, get in line, and hold your glass at just the right angle to catch a few fingers of cider from that hissing stream. You drink the small amount in your glass and then follow the cider maker to the next barrel.

Thinking it was a free-for-all, my first faux pas was coming at the stream from the wrong side and essentially butting in line. Then, I couldn't quite figure out how to hold my glass so that the cider hit at the right angle, to "break" the liquid and create foam. Thankfully, the crowd at the Basque cider house was very forgiving. A kind white-haired man in a sweater, whose group was eating next to us, showed me the ropes, hopping up and waving me along with him at the next shout of "txotx!"

We quickly learned that advice was forthcoming if you sought it out. At a cider house in the town center, called Zapiain, a hand-painted mural of "don'ts" was on the wall: don't cut in line; don't fill your glass all the way up; don't sit on the barrels. Tyler grasped the technique much quicker than I did.

"Here, take it here, at an angle," said Igór, our tour guide at Petritegi, another sagardotegi just down the road from Gartziategi (the suffix *tegi* means "place of"). I did as Igór said, allowing the stream to hit the very rim of my glass, spraying a little bit on the floor, just as the locals do. (I got the hang of it on my fourth glass.) Some older sagardotegi actually have grooves worn in the cement floors from years of streaming cider. The point, Igór told us, was to make sure the cider has good *txinparta*, or foam; if the cider is healthy, that foam should dissipate quickly. The cider in the glass disappears quickly, too. The flavors are funky, crisp and acidic, and usually bone dry—nothing like so many of the cloying, over-carbonated ciders you too often find on draft at home.

In late January, Astigarraga was still relatively mellow. But as txotx season rolls on, more than 15,000 cider enthusiasts can crowd into the town's cider houses each weekend. Txotx season follows the apple harvest of September and October, then fermentation of the cider in early winter. In fact, in late January, some of the barrels might not be fully finished fermentation. "The cider in the barrel is still evolving," Igór said. "If you come back in two months and taste the same barrel, it will have evolved." In Basque Country, most cider is made by spontaneous fermentation and no added commercial yeast, similar to natural winemaking. Once the season ends in April, whatever's left in the barrel is bottled.

The annual ritual hearkens back to an era when cider makers would invite clients, perhaps innkeepers, restaurateurs, or the famed gastronomic societies of San Sebastián, to taste and choose which casks they wanted to purchase. "Here, cider is not just an alcoholic beverage," Igór said. "It's a way of life." Petritegi, for instance, dates to 1526.

Over the years, a meal became part of the ritual. Every cider house serves the same basic menu for 30 euros: chorizo; cod omelet; roasted cod with green peppers; thick, medium-rare chuleta steak; Basque cheese (such as Idiazabal) served with walnuts and membrillo. And all the cider you can drink. We were served roughly the same dishes in all seven cider houses we visited. "Twenty years ago, there were no chairs," Igór said. "The food was just served in the middle of the table." For three of the cider houses we visited, they still did not offer chairs and we stood to eat. Petritegi did indeed offer chairs—and a beautiful hake in garlic and oil as an alternative to the cod. But Petritegi is a bit more contemporary, perhaps because of its partnership with Shacksbury, which imports its Espumosa bottling made in the Champagne method.

The cider house ritual is just one of many Basque Country cultural touchstones that make this autonomous coastal region a very different place from the rest of the Spain. In Astigarraga, a sleepy but pleasant town, we took a lovely, steep, and tiring hike up to an old church that had been a stop on the ancient Camino de Santiago pilgrimage. As we wandered past orchards overlooking the bay of San Sebastián, our guide, Ainize, told us stories of the Basque golden age. In the 16th century, Basque ships were built around the cider barrels, and each sailor drank up to three liters of cider per day to fend off scurvy. The result, according to lore, was that the Basque fishermen and whale hunters were the healthiest and most renowned on the sea, fishing far from their home waters. Their range was so legendary that, only two years ago, the remote West Fjörds of Iceland repealed a 400-year-old law that ordered the murder of any Basque visitor on sight.

"The 16th century was the golden age of cider, but cider making is much older than that," Ainize said. "The original meaning of *txotx*, in our language, is 'to speak.' Now it's an invitation to drink cider."

As we descended back into the town square, Ainize pointed out the local pelota court, where a traditional handball game is played. Many believe that this sport originated with the ancient Greeks. We also saw huge stones with handles that are used for lifting and carrying in another Basque sport. The day before, we drank cider with a woman named Olatz who told us, "I carry a stone of 550 kilos with eight women." She added, with a laugh: "We have our own sports here."

At Petritegi, Igór took us through the orchards where we learned about Basque varieties of apples like Goikoetxe, Moko, Txalaka, Gezamina, and Urtebi—we were far away from Golden Russet, Rhode Island Greening, or Northern Spy. A Basque cider can be made from more than a hundred varieties—mostly bittersharps and bittersweets—and 40 to 50 might be blended in a single cider. We were told that one kilo of apples will make one bottle. We were also told by a number of people that apples are sometimes trucked in from Normandy or Galicia to keep up with demand.

In the town center, Sidrería Bereziartua operates a tasting room, and so we booked a tasting. "Cider is deep in our culture," said Mikel, our pourer. "We don't even know when we started making it." Ciders using the official denomination of origin, Euskal Sagardoa, created in 2016, must be made entirely from Basque apples. When he poured Bereziartua's Euskal Sagardoa, Mikel said, "If you want to take one bottle, drink this one." Then he poured a cider with a Gorenak label, one that can use foreign apples in the blend—but still must adhere to strict standards and be approved by official tasters. "If you want to drink three bottles, you take this one," he said. Buying bottles at the cider houses in Basque Country is relatively inexpensive. I never saw a 750-mililiter bottle priced above 10 euros, and most were under five euros.

On our last evening, we went to Lizeaga, a sagardotegi in a 16th-century farmhouse that's next to Gartziategi. Earlier, our stone-carrying friend Olatz had described the house as "the real txotx." Our reservation at one of the long tables was marked with a baguette. There were no chairs. After the opening plate of chorizo, we strolled into the barrel room. Gabriel, the cider maker, was opening the ancient taps with what looked like pliers. Gabriel went from cask to cask, and we followed along, dashing back into the dining room in between for the omelet, the cod, the steak.

After the eighth or ninth (or 10th?) txotx, and after some debating of technique with my brother, I thought I had finally gotten the catch down like a true Basque. But on the next txotx, when I put my glass under the stream, Gabriel gently corrected my form: "No, no," he said, "have the cider hit here." Well, no matter. Soon enough he tapped another barrel, and there was another chance to learn.

CHAPTER 9
THE WINTER MEETINGS

Once I returned home from Spain, the deep winter of 2018 had set in, with record low temperatures throughout the Northeast. Unlike in Basque Country, where January kicked off a raucous, festive cider season, winter on the American cider calendar is a time for serious thinking and contemplation. The apples have been picked and pressed months ago, and now the juice sits in stainless steel tanks, quietly fermenting. Thoughts in the cider community turn to the future, and to bigger picture issues. So as January flipped into February, I traveled to Baltimore to attend the annual CiderCon, hosted by the United States Association of Cider Makers, a trade group with more than 1,000 members.

I've been to many drinks conferences, such as the infamously debaucherous Tales of the Cocktail in New Orleans, attended by thousands of bartenders, where the "education" was generally delivered in between a multitude of free cocktails, swag, and giveaway bottles. After a few tipsy seminars and tastings, there's something like the Beefeater's Gin Welcome Party, followed by the Absolut Vodka Party (where Absolut launches some ridiculous new flavored vodka), followed by the Hendrick's Gin After Party. I vaguely remember one "educational" session, after midnight, that was served by women whose naked bodies were painted blue, and another rye whiskey product launch that happened inside Hustler's Barely Legal Club on Bourbon Street.

CiderCon is decidedly not like this. When I checked in at the Marriott in Baltimore's Inner Harbor, I received a lanyard and a swag bag that contained a package of Fermentis SafCider Yeast for Cider Production, along with the conference agenda.

Defining "cider"—and creating a language to talk about it—was very much on the USACM's agenda in 2018. Only a few months before, the association had released its Cider Style Guide, the one that first delineated the "modern" versus "heritage" divide for cider. But there were other specialty style categories established as well, including fruit ciders, hopped ciders, spiced ciders, wood-aged ciders, ice ciders, and—possibly to the disdain of Ryan Burk at Angry Orchard—sour ciders. The Cider Style Guide had been the product of a great deal of heated debate and hand-wringing among the membership, and the various presenters and stakeholders at CiderCon danced cautiously around the issue of modern versus heritage.

"We had to find a way to organize the messy world of cider," said Eric West, publisher of Cider Guide, who'd helped create the Style Guide.

"It's very inclusive," said Paul Vander Heide, owner of Vander Mill Cider in Michigan, and a USACM board member. "We have such a small market share, we can't afford to exclude anyone."

"We hear consumers say, 'I've had a cider. I don't like cider.' But they don't realize how vast the category is," said Michelle McGrath, the association's executive director. "You can have a hopped apricot cider made from dessert apples, and you can have a bone-dry sparkling cider made from cider or heirloom varieties. People value a wine grape, and we're trying to get people to value a cider apple."

"We want to have a big tent," said Brian Rutzen, from The Northman in Chicago.

The desire for a big tent is understandable. At the keynote breakfast session, a guy from Nielsen, the ratings and market research company, told the crowd that four percent of American consumers say that cider is their "adult beverage of choice." This is up from about one percent a decade ago. At another session, Burk talked about a recent Google poll of 21- to 35-year-olds in which they were asked, "Can you name a cider brand?" About half of those polled could not name a single cider brand. Nine percent of those surveyed named Angry Orchard. Another 20 percent named brands that are not actually ciders at all: Mike's Hard Lemonade and Redd's Apple Ale. Clearly, there's work to be done.

I attended a training class for the newly created Certified Cider Professional program. At that point, I was so deep into cider that I'd decided I would soon take the exam for the CCP credential. Even at this study session, in a ballroom packed with more than 100 CCP hopefuls, the modern versus heritage divide caused a lot of consternation.

A team of cider people, including West, Rutzen, Vander Heide, and author Darlene Hayes, taught the class. The PowerPoint slides on apple history, genetics, orchards, presses, and cider making all seemed straightforward. We learned that apples originated in Central Asia, that pear cider is called perry, that apples can be sweet, sharp, bittersweet, or bittersharp, that Golden Russet, Newtown Pippin, Northern Spy, and Harrison are heirloom apples. Then we got to the Style Guide. And then things got a little more complicated.

Heritage ciders, according to the slide, were described as having "increased complexity" and "complex aromatics," which caused some grumbling in the audience. "We use the word *complex* a lot. But I don't want to make this a value judgment," Rutzen said. But if heritage ciders are *complex*, someone in the audience wanted to know, does that mean that modern ciders are *simple*?

"I don't want to say simple," West said. "But we're struggling with language."

When we got to the category of sour ciders, Rutzen—who had been on the contentious Spanish-style sidra panel at Cider Days—said, "Sour evokes, um, different reactions."

During the section about specialty ciders, someone in the audience raised her hand. "So with the style guidelines, where would a rhubarb cider go?" she asked. "It's not a fruit. It's not a spice." The team of teachers looked at one another, stumped.

Another person raised his hand. "The term *heirloom apple* has come up a lot. But what's our definition of an heirloom apple?" Again, the teachers looked at one another. Hayes finally said, definitively, "Older varieties that are not widely found in the supermarkets today." Then she added: "But the definition is evolving." In fact, as I was finishing this book in December 2018, the USACM introduced five brand-new cider styles, including a "botanical" category (presumably where rhubarb will now go) and two rosé cider categories, modern rosé and heritage rosé (the latter must be made with red-fleshed apples).

Rutzen suggested that, in the end, all cider styles boil down to the cider maker's intention. "Make your choices and be smart," he said. "This is America. Do what you want. But you'll have to live with the consequences."

There was almost palpable relief in the room when the team moved on to sections on evaluating flavor in cider ("evaluating a cider is much like evaluating a wine") and on food pairings ("match strength with strength; think blue cheese and ice cider").

* * *

One evening, at an event called Cider Share (a popular name for cider events, apparently) 50 producers poured their ciders and I sampled dozens from across the country. There were certainly heritage producers on hand, like Black Diamond from the Finger Lakes, next to upstart heritage producers such as Milk + Honey or Keepsake from Minnesota and Anxo in DC. But, by and large, the modern style of cider reigned. I tasted lots of hopped ciders, ciders spiced with ginger or pepper, or flavored with black currant or tart cherry or raspberry—all falling into the association's various categories. Plenty of producers made both modern and heritage. Tandem Cider from northern Michigan, for instance, had a delicious single-varietal McIntosh poured next to one that used mostly the heirloom Rhode Island Greening variety, both in cans.

At the table of Noble Cider, from Asheville, North Carolina, I chatted with cider maker Trevor Baker, an association board member who aggressively identifies as a modern cider producer. Among his flavored offerings, Baker poured me a cranberry-orange cider, spiced with habanero pepper. "The habanero is not so much a flavoring as a chest warmer," Baker said. I didn't know quite what to say after tasting it. I certainly could not discern an apple. Not my cup of tea.

A cider blogger whom I recognized from an earlier session approached Noble's table, and Baker shouted, "How'd you like to taste a hopped peach cider?"

"Hell, yes," she said. "I love ciders with stone fruit."

In contrast to the Cider Share, I attended a panel called "Heritage Cider: Keys to Success in the Next Growth Category." Autumn Stoscheck from Eve's and Sam Fitz from Anxo were on the panel, along with Diane Flynt, a legendary apple grower from Appalachian Virginia who recently retired from producing her Foggy Ridge Cider. Flynt opened the session with an image of old-school evangelical church with a sign reading: REPENT. Flynt's message was simple: The cider industry needed to move away from modern cider and focus on heritage. "You may have to repent," she said. "You may have to have a mind change. Making this kind of cider is so much different than just changing your ingredients. But you can do it. Or, if you just want to get it into a keg and sell it, then you can just take Peter Mitchell's 5-day cider class and then go off and make cider."

Cider is certainly a messy, chaotic, and growing space—that's what makes it dynamic. But Flynt's assertion is that, as the category matures, what will most likely appeal to the gatekeepers who stock store shelves and create bar menus, as well as to knowledgeable drinks aficionados, is going to be heritage cider. "The most talented and important beverage professionals in the nation want this kind of cider," she said. "Your most sophisticated customers want this kind of cider. Consumers are not dumb. They know the difference between Yellow Tail and Châteauneuf-du-Pape."

With the mention of the famed Rhône wine, Autumn said, "I believe cider can achieve the same depth and complexity."

"Yes," Flynt said. "But no winemaker would start by saying, 'Where can I find the cheapest riesling'?"

Autumn was also on a panel called "Champagne Method Cider," where I experienced several mind-blowing sparkling ciders, made with such varieties as Kingston Black, Yarlington Mill, Dabinett, Somerset Redstreak, and foraged wild crab apples by Eden Specialty Ciders in Vermont, Snowdrift Cider in Washington State, as well as Redbyrd and Autumn's own Eve's Cidery from the Finger Lakes. In this hotel ballroom, far from the orchard, they were yet another reminder that cider is every bit as complex as fine wine. Questions from the audience about aging on the lees, the use of barrels, and malolactic fermentation made it feel more like a wine event. Tim Larsen, from Snowdrift, even paraphrased the old wine-making cliché: "Cider making, as everyone here agrees, begins in the orchard."

"Making cider this way is very expensive," said Autumn. "But when you can buy a traditional-method sparkling cider made from beautiful fruit like this for under $20, that's a great value." It's true that few sparkling wines would rival, say, Redbyrd's $27 Celeste Sur Lie, bone dry with a creaminess balanced by elegant tannins and razor-sharp acidity. When someone in the audience raved about his cider, Eric Shatt from Redbyrd shrugged and said, "Well, we never have a shortage of acid in the Finger Lakes."

These were surely specialty bottlings, representing a small part of each producer's business. "Who is this for and how do you market it?" said Eden cider maker Eleanor Léger, repeating a question from the audience. "My first thought is: 'I have no effing clue.'"

With so many swirling and competing visions of cider, between modern and heritage, big and small, it's no surprise that confusion occasionally reigned. During a session titled "Wild Fermentation and Other Heritage Cider Options," we tasted ciders from hip, in-the-know producers like the Hudson Valley's Sundström, as well as bottlings from Angry Orchard's Innovation Cider House and E.Z. Orchards from Oregon. "It's about imparting less of my desires on the final product," Leif Sundström told the audience.

"Cider making is all about choices," we were told by Tom Oliver, a legendary cider maker from Herefordshire, England, renowned for his wild, pungent, complex ciders. "I think wild ferment is a good choice. It's more complex, more character building. It's all about context. You need to know what you're trying to achieve. The clue for me is the word *wild*. If you're doing wild then there's an embrace of whatever will happen will happen."

As we all tasted the funky, tannic ciders, an apple grower from Tyro, Virginia, named Adam Cooke, stood up and expressed genuine confusion. "I'm at the point where I can plant 20 acres of bittersweet apple varieties," Cooke said. "But what I want to know: Is this just a passing trend? Will there be a demand in 10 years?" The crowd quieted awkwardly. It was as if Cooke had audibly farted in the middle of the room.

Ryan Burk, the cider maker at Angry Orchard, glared at him and admonished him, saying: "Be part of what makes it happen. There's a different market for Concord grapes and pinot noir."

Later, I saw Cooke, who owns Silver Creek & Seaman's Orchard, and chatted with him. A few days later, he clarified his position via email: "I must say I am a little put off by some of the skinny-jean bearded pretentiousness of it." He called the wild fermentation panel "a hell of an example of hard cider veering into the wrong direction" and said, "I don't understand this allure of UK-style cider that reeks of old cheese and stinky feet. We threw the king off the property nearly 250 years ago." But what concerned Cooke the most was the potential effect on apple farmers like him. "In less than ten years supply will outweigh demand and the American farmer who invested heavily in planting English varieties and cider apples will suffer," he wrote. "I watched it happen to hop farmers."

I ran into Sam Fitz of Anxo in the bar of the Marriott hotel. Baltimore, less than an hour from Washington, is home turf for Anxo, and the bar here was stocked with its Cidre Blanc. We cracked open two cans and talked. Even though he is relatively new to the scene, Fitz had already won a seat on the USACM board. "The West Coast producers aren't too cool with the 'heritage' moniker," he told me.

Fitz sources a lot of his apples from Adam Cooke in Virginia, and we talked about Cooke's concerns. Like many others, Fitz believes the future of cider lies in convincing larger apple growers like Cooke to invest in cider and heirloom apple varieties and larger cideries to move away from using dessert apples. Right now, by most estimates, only about 10 percent of cideries in the nation have their own orchards. "We have to get back to cider apples, heirloom apples," he said. "How many Anxos can exist? There just aren't that many cider apples available."

As we drank his Cidre Blanc—made from eating apples and served in a can, but certainly artisan or craft or "heritage" in intention—Fitz said, "The industry is still trying to figure itself out. We don't really know who our market is. And I think we have to create a moment for cider. It's all up in the air right now." But in the lobby bar, in freezing cold Baltimore, as hundreds of cider people buzzed around us, he added: "Whatever cider is going to become, it is being decided right now."

Throughout CiderCon, I'd run into Steve Selin, from South Hill in the Finger Lakes. At the Cider Share, he seemed completely overwhelmed by the throngs of people squeezing up to tables to be poured modern cider. Afterward, we decided to have a quiet dinner away from the conference. We went to a red-sauce Italian restaurant in Fells Point, along with a couple of Black Diamond's cider makers, and Michael Phillips, the soft-spoken and bearded owner of Lost Nation Orchard in New Hampshire and author of *The Holistic Orchard*, a seminal book on organic fruit growing. At dinner, there was a debate over whether or not stressing an apple tree resulted in better fruit for cider. The benefit of stressing a tree in growing conditions where it struggles was something Autumn Stoscheck had first suggested to me as we walked her Albee Hill orchard. Now, Phillips was asked: Did he believe in stressing apple trees? "Well," Phillips said, "I do want to let the tree experience environmental realities." Phillips asked Selin, "Have you ever grafted a wild apple?" When he answered yes, Phillips asked, "Did you name it?"

"I call it Dawes Melody," Selin said. "It's the road name plus the name of the woman who owns the farm." Everyone nodded their heads and smiled. This discussion felt a million miles away from Style Guides and market share and modern cider. Later that night, we went to a crowded special event in Fells Point where Anxo and Angry Orchard were pouring special bottlings. Selin ended up playing euchre in a corner of the bar with some others from the Finger Lakes.

The next evening, Selin told me that he was skipping the cider-industry events. He was crashing on the couch of some friends he knew from the Americana and bluegrass scene (and his days as a violinmaker) and he invited me over to listen to them play music. I arrived at the home, in a Baltimore neighborhood that looked straight out of *The Wire*. Inside, Selin and three others tuned up their instruments—a couple of fiddles, a banjo, and a guitar—as we drank South Hill Packbasket. Selin and the other musicians sat close to one another in the living room, watching each other's fingerpicking, improvising as they went along, riffing on old American folk chords and melodies they all knew by heart. Right as they began playing, a young, pierced, and tattooed woman arrived, slipped on clogs and started Appalachian flatfoot dancing. I closed my eyes and listened. I remembered something Selin had once told me: "In those old Americana songs, they weren't singing about beer and whiskey. They sang about cider and whiskey."

* * *

There's a recurring nightmare for purveyors of certain high-end fermented beverages. An enthusiastic customer is served this drink for the first time. The customer is told that it is "dry." Or at least it's mostly dry. Or at least there's a lot of acidity that "balances" the sweetness. The customer's smile becomes a raised eyebrow of confusion. After a sip or two, he or she declares: "It's too sweet. I don't like it." And just like that, with those simple, almost childlike words, an entire drinks category is dead to that consumer.

Riesling pops to mind as one of those categories. A few years back, there was a whole riesling revival going on. Remember the Summers of Riesling of the late 2000s and early 2010s when bars were geeking out over the grape? Sadly, there was much confusion. Even though there are many riesling styles, from bone-dry to dessert, too many consumers perceived the wine as only sweet. Ironically, by the height of the trendy revival, riesling sales were actually declining.

Now along comes the American cider revival, with cider having its own riesling-like moment. And those who promote cider are hearing a frustratingly familiar refrain: I don't like cider. It's too sweet. "It's the number one issue for cider," said Michelle McGrath, the USACM executive director. "People are assuming that ciders are much more sweet than they are."

For that reason, the USACM was pushing forward with discussions on how to create a universal dryness scale that cider makers can put on their labels, designating whether the cider inside is dry, semi-dry, semi-sweet, or sweet. The problem is getting a bunch of human beings to agree to a definition of what, precisely, "sweetness" or "dryness" means. Can sweetness be measured simply by testing how much residual sugar remains after fermentation? Or do factors such as acidity affect how people perceive sweetness in their mouths?

One potential scale that's currently being debated by cider makers around the country was developed by the New York State Cider Association. Ironically, it is based on a scale adopted in 2008 by the International Riesling Foundation. "People are abusing the word *dry* and will continue to. We can't stop that," said Jenn Smith, executive director of the NYCA. "But New York is going to adopt this scale whether or not the rest of the country does."

The Orchard-Based Cider Dryness Scale proposed by NYCA takes into account three factors in assessing perceived sweetness: residual sugar, acidity, and tannins. A particular cider might have eight grams per liter of residual sugar—which sounds "sweet." But if that cider also has seven grams per liter of malic acid, and 700 parts per million of tannins . . . well, that's going to be perceived as very dry. Meanwhile a cider with less residual sugar, but very low acid and fewer tannins, is going to be perceived as semi-dry or even sweet. OK, yes, for those like me, who got a C in chemistry, this sort of formula may feel a little complicated. But there's a logic and science behind it: All of these factors can be tested and corroborated in a sensory analysis lab.

Cider makers in New York's Finger Lakes such as Redbyrd, Kite & String, and Black Diamond have already been using a version of this scale on their back labels, and there is support among a number of well-known producers throughout the Northeast. When I open a cider using this scale, I'm rarely, if ever, surprised by the level of dryness or sweetness.

But there's been resistance to the Orchard-Based Cider Dryness Scale in other regions. "The New York folks fired the first salvo, but it rubbed a lot of people the wrong way," said Eric West, the publisher of Cider Guide, who was on the team who taught the Certified Cider Professional class. West is also director of the Great Lakes Cider and Perry Competition (GLINTCAP), the world's largest cider judging body. GLINTCAP already uses a dryness/sweetness scale for its judging categories based solely on residual sugar, using guidelines similar to the European Union—with anything under 9 grams of residual sugar classified as "dry."

Dryness scales have become part of a larger discussion about the lexicon of cider as well the modern versus heritage divide. Since heritage ciders use more traditional bittersweet or bittersharp cider apples, older heirloom varieties or perhaps even crab apples or foraged wild varieties, those are usually going to have more acidity or tannins. A simple reason why many cider makers don't like New

York's Orchard-Based Cider Dryness Scale is because in many parts of the country, they make modern ciders from dessert apples that do not have much in the way of tannins or acidity. Another reason for the pushback has been that the New York scale only takes into account ciders made from 100 percent apples or other pome fruit. So all those popular modern ciders with added ingredients like hops, berries, juniper, tea, ginger—and cranberry-orange-habanero—would not qualify.

Finally, there's still the large contingent of cider makers who have grown out of the craft beer industry and are deeply skeptical of a wine-based approach. Besides, asks Mike Reis, host of the cider podcast Redfield Radio, how well does complex nomenclature work for, say, German riesling? "How many people walk into a wine shop and understand what *trockenbeerenauslese* means?"

* * *

In late February, I was back in the Finger Lakes, for the annual meeting of the New York Cider Association. Cider makers from all over New York gathered inside the Finger Lakes Cider House on a cold sunny afternoon. Here, Jenn Smith, the NYCA's executive director, and Ian Merwin from Black Diamond introduced the proposed Orchard-Based Cider Dryness Scale to a crowd of about 50 people. "We want to call this orchard-based. There's a subtext. We want to sustain a cider industry," said Merwin. He suggested that the cider community's current "big tent" philosophy was a "weird situation"—with heritage producers promoted next to producers using concentrate and selling flavors like cranberry-orange-habanero. "If we were the wine industry, it would be like if we allowed people to use Thompson Seedless or Concord grapes, and then add adjuncts," he said. At the same time, Merwin said that the Orchard-Based Cider Dryness Scale would not be a panacea, especially since they only had a tiny budget. "We're not capable of policing this nationwide," he said.

The discussion of the dryness scale was followed by a group exercise in brainstorming words that represent the "brand identity of New York cider." Words like *tradition, authenticity, orchard,* and even *terroir* were suggested. After that, a guy who exported cider to Japan made a sales pitch, followed by a presentation by Cornell University researcher Gregory Peck. Peck had recently visited the British cider market and presented his comparative study. While the US cider market is more than $1 billion, the market in the UK is more than $4 billion. A key difference is that 80 percent of the apples used in British cider production are either bittersharp or bittersweet apple varieties. "The problem in the US is that our cider apples come from culinary orchards." While New York has a leg up on other regions because there are a lot of heirloom varieties like Golden Russet and Northern Spy, the big question moving forward for the state's apple growers remains, according to Peck: "Do we plant cider apples? Is it profitable to grow cider apples in New York State?"

Finally, Bill Pitt of Wafler Nursery stepped to the podium. Wafler Nursery, founded in 1962 on Lake Ontario, is one of the state's largest purveyors of fruit trees, growing about 800,000 trees per year. Though he sells varieties like Dabinett, Chisel Jersey, Yarlington Mill, and Porter's Perfection, Pitt talked about how much he disliked cider apple trees. For the grower, he said, "there's nothing good about these varieties." He listed all the problems these cider-apple trees faced: they're late blooming; they're susceptible to fire blight; they have variable, inconsistent size. "Some have very strange growth habits," Pitt said. Growers, he said, prefer disease-resistant culinary varieties. One particularly troublesome apple for Pitt is Kingston Black, so coveted among cider people for single-varietal bottlings. "I think Kingston Black is the worst variety you could grow," he said. "I know you cider guys love it. But I hate it."

The following day, the NYCA hosted a Cider Tasting and Sensory Education for Apple Growers, sponsored in part by Angry Orchard. A dozen or so growers showed up at Blue Barn Cidery, about 20 minutes north of Rochester near Lake Ontario for the event. The goal was simple: to convince these growers to plant more cider and heirloom apples by showing them the difference those varieties make in the glass. Jenn Smith, Ian Merwin, and Chris Gerling from Cornell University's Enology Extension Lab gave the presentation.

Gerling showed slides on the "Impact of Tannins and Acidity on Perceived Dryness" and explained the effects of sweetness, astringency, bitterness, and tannins on how drinkers perceive flavor. "Flavor is very difficult to define," he said.

Merwin led everyone through a tasting of 10 ciders. We tasted samples made from Idared, a dessert variety, next to samples made from acidic Northern Spy and tannic Chisel Jersey. Then we tasted Eve's Cidery's Autumn's Gold, with dozens of varieties blended. Merwin poured several of his Black Diamond ciders, both dry and medium-dry to show the difference that residual sugar makes. I raised my hand and asked him about the minerality in his Slate-Stone. He stopped me and said, "No, we're not getting into that today."

Once we had tasted through the 10 ciders, and lunch was about to be served, Merwin told the audience, "When I say high-quality cider, I mean something that people will pay wine-like prices for." At that point, the issue of apple prices was finally explored. If the tasting didn't convince the growers to take an interest in these varieties, perhaps price would. The current wholesale price for basic juice-grade culinary apples is about five cents per pound. Compare that to 25 cents per pound for heirlooms and 45 cents per pound for bittersweet and bittersharp cider varieties. "There's an unmet demand for cider apples," Smith told them.

* * *

The day after the tasting at Blue Barn Cidery, I visited with John Reynolds at Blackduck Cidery. Reynolds, predictably, had not attended CiderCon or the meeting of the NYCA, of which he was not a member. "I'm an anarchist," he said. "Why would I belong to that group? Angry Orchard is behind the scenes giving them money, right? Aren't they going to have a bigger voice than mine?"

Unsurprisingly, he was not supportive of the proposed dryness scale. "It's nonsense! If we're going to do this, where is the enforcement? Everyone lies!" He suggested random testing if the industry wanted "a real seal of truth."

Reynolds had just gotten his annual supply of scion wood, new cuttings from trees at the USDA agricultural experiment station in Geneva, and the twigs were piled up in his tasting room. He'd be grafting these to rootstock during the springtime. This year, he'd requested several Spanish varieties and some rare varieties from Kazakhstan. He'd been looking for more drought-resistant trees and figured trees from a semi-desert climate like Kazakhstan might make sense. "Plus Kazakhstan is clearly where the apple originated," he said. He also got several new varieties of crab apples to plant.

I asked him why he didn't get any English or French varieties, like so many other cider orchardists. "Those varieties have too many issues here," he said. He believes many of the popular cider-apple trees are too susceptible to fire blight and to slip into biennial production. "English and French varieties are not the future here," he said. "That's the problem with telling growers to grow these." Crab apples in the Finger Lakes, Reynolds believes, will become a more consistent source of acidity and tannins for cider. This is indeed a minority opinion. "But remember, I'm always the black sheep of the Finger Lakes cider community," he said.

Several of Reynold's new ciders had finished fermentation, and we tasted some tank samples. One in particular was a delicious new blend, called Three Bears, of pears, apples, and quince. Then we tasted the wild perry by itself. This vintage had an even more pronounced green note of sage and celery. When I told Reynolds this, he said, "I had a restaurant guy in here the other day that called that flavor lovage. Lovage!" We both laughed. "Now that's a douchey wine term," he said.

CHAPTER 10
THE JUDGMENT OF GRAND RAPIDS

I don't know what it says about the state of cider, but just 15 months after my first visit to Wassail and the beginning of my journey, I was invited to be a judge at the 13th annual Great Lakes International Cider and Perry Competition, known as GLINTCAP, the world's largest cider competition. I was still a couple of months from taking the Certified Cider Professional exam, and I definitely felt a tinge of impostor syndrome. But my wine book had just been published a month before, and I'd been on a mini book tour, doing readings, interviews, and random events—I'd just judged a cocktail competition in Rochester a few weeks before, for instance. I guess I was feeling cocky enough to believe that I was prepared to judge just about any beverage. So on a warm May evening, I arrived at the Gerald R. Ford Airport in Grand Rapids, Michigan, where GLINTCAP happens each spring.

I checked into my hotel, next to the Gerard R. Ford Presidential Library & Museum, and then walked across a bridge over the Grand River to find a late dinner and a beer—I figured I'd be sipping enough cider over the next few days and I knew that Grand Rapids is often voted Beer City USA, with more than 60 craft breweries. On my walk, I passed the Amway Grand Plaza, the DeVos Place Convention Center, and the DeVos Performance Hall (the father-in-law of our Secretary of Education, Betsy DeVos, is the billionaire founder of Amway, the pyramid selling company, which is based in the suburbs). Most everything was closed at that hour, but I found one bar that was pouring Founders and Bell's—two of Michigan's famed craft beers—over loud karaoke performances, including one guy with tight pants and a scarf who appeared to be channeling Axl Rose.

The next morning I went on a bus tour, organized so the judges and GLINTCAP volunteers could visit local orchards and cideries. We traversed what is known as the Fruit Ridge (or The Ridge)—an eight-mile-wide and 20-mile-long area north of Grand Rapids, about 25 miles from Lake Michigan—one of the great fruit-growing regions in the world. Michigan ranks just behind Washington and New York as the nation's third-largest apple-growing region, and a majority of those apples come from The Ridge's fertile clay and loam soils, at elevations of more than 800 feet. I was thrilled for the chance to see the cider country of Michigan, which has nearly as many cideries as New York.

About three dozen of us boarded the bus, along with our tour guide, Mike Beck, cider maker of nearby Uncle John's Cider Mill. It was a mix of professional and amateur cider makers from around the US, some beverage directors, and a few cider writers. The morning began with cider and doughnuts at the Peoples Cider Company in downtown Grand Rapids. "I normally hate cider and doughnuts, but today it seems like the right thing," said Jason Lümmen, the cider maker at the Peoples Cider, who had a shaved mohawk and long beard and wore a black T-shirt that read "Stop Glorifying Rats." Peoples Cider had hopped and ginger ciders, and was experimenting with a number of barrel agings—The Flying Dutchmen, aged in brandy barrels and made with bittersharps and bittersweets, was particularly good. However, Lümmen told the group, "I'm not really chasing the English varieties like a lot of people in this industry."

After a quick tasting, we were back on the bus, rolling up to The Ridge. It was a beautiful sunny spring day, with a wide blue sky, and we passed miles and miles of blossoming fruit trees. We were a festive group on the bus. I sat next to an amateur cider maker named Peter Milner who foraged wild crab apples in Nova Scotia. In front of me were two winemakers from Michigan's Leelanau Peninsula, north of Traverse City, who were considering a move into cider. I had a heated, but good-natured, debate over East Coast versus West Coast cider styles with Christine Walter, the head cider maker at Bauman's Cider Company in Portland, Oregon. A guy named Ronald LaPorte told me about his Patriots' Heritage cider, which he'd just started in Schaghticoke, New York, near Albany. LaPorte told me, "I'm not targeting the cider drinker, I'm targeting the spirits drinker." He was aging cider in all kinds of barrels, including one that previously stored peaty Laphroig scotch. "How do you reach drinkers over 40?" he wanted to know. I had no idea, and I understood his frustration. While people in their 20s and 30s were embracing cider, for some reason, the most difficult to convert were the 40-somethings of my own generation.

The bus stopped at Robinette's Apple Haus & Winery, where we met the Robinette brothers: Ed, 59; Bill, 53; John, 49. They loaded all of us into an open trailer and pulled us by tractor through their 45-acre orchard, where they grow more than 40 apple varieties. The Robinettes' orchards have been here since 1911, and the Apple Haus is a local institution—the kind of place where you can bring the kids for sweet cider, U-Pick apples, tractor rides, a corn maze, a petting zoo, ice cream, and cider doughnuts. As old as the orchards are, the Robinettes only began making true cider about 12 years ago. The brothers told us that they'd committed to planting cider apple trees about five years ago. "So we were a little ahead of the curve," Bill said.

"Or a little behind the curve by about a hundred years," Ed said.

"We don't even know what some of these varieties are going to look like," Bill said. Both Bill and Ed also expressed worry over fire blight and other fungal diseases, which attack the trees worst during the spring bloom. The Robinettes' worries were similar to those of revivalists all over America who were staking their business on growing apple varieties for cider. The future was both exciting and terrifying.

After Robinette's, the bus tour stopped for lunch at Vander Mill Cider, where we were greeted by owner Paul Vander Heide, the USACM board member who had helped teach the Certified Cider Professional course at CiderCon. Vander Mill is a major player in the Midwest, where you'll find it on cider menus in Chicago and other cities. Vander Mill's ciders veer toward semi-dry and modern, but they're well made, with good structure. During lunch, I enjoyed Vander Mill's Chapman's Blend (named after Johnny Appleseed), made with Winesap, Baldwin, and Northern Spy, as well as its Bon Chretien perry ("Good Christian" was the original name of the Bartlett Pear). But the best, for my taste, was the Casnovia, unfiltered and barrel fermented from Dabinett, Yarlington Mill, Golden Russet, and Esopus Spitzenburg. Vander Mill's many different dry and semi-dry offerings are just the sort of ciders that would benefit from an accurate sweetness scale as was discussed all winter. There's nothing wrong with ciders that have some residual sugar—as long as consumers understand what they're getting and can find what they want. Whether too dry or too sweet, all it takes is one misleading glass for a drinker to shut down a whole category.

After lunch, we stopped at Ridge Cider Co., a modern cidery that poured flavors like Peach Ridge, Blue-Nana, and strawberry-flavored Strawdogg. One called Porchsitting was flavored with cinnamon and vanilla. Someone asked about a cider listed as Rooster. "Oh, that's got coffee in it," said the guy pouring. Peter Milner, the forager from Nova Scotia, asked, "Do you have anything that's just got apples?"

"As you all know, it's not easy to find those cider apples," said Matt Delong, Ridge's founder. "But we're trying our best."

Finally, we ended up at Schaefer Orchards, which makes Pux Cider. The orchards have been in the Schaefer family since the 1850s. But in 2012, the family planted a number of heirlooms, bittersharps, and bittersweets for cider, led by the younger generation, brothers Chris and Andy. By now, they're cultivating more than 125 varieties. "Uncle Mark" took the group on a tour amid the blossoming rows of trees he'd grafted from scion wood—Stoke Red, Tremletts Bitters, Spitzenburg, Northern Spy, and crab apples similar to many orchards back East. Inside, the Schaefer brothers—Chris with dreadlocks pulled back into a ponytail, and Andy, bald with a long beard and mustache—poured ciders from the tap that ranged from a barrel-aged offering flavored with tart cherry to one flavored with blood orange to an amazing 2015 vintage simply called Harvest that was a wild-fermented blend of foraged apples, heirlooms, bittersweets, and even some dessert fruit. "That's the last keg," said Andy. This was a serious, dry, delicious cider.

As we all gathered back on the bus, and returned to Grand Rapids, I cracked open a can of Jak, the Schaeffer brothers' single-varietal Northern Spy. I was realizing that Michigan's cider culture existed somewhere between East and West, between heritage and modern.

* * *

Once the bus tour got back to Grand Rapids that evening, there was a mandatory training seminar for all judges at the conference Marriott. Several dozen more judges joined us at crowded tables in the hotel ballroom, and the session was led by Charles McGonegal, cider maker at ÆppelTreow (pronounced "apple true") in Wisconsin, and GLINTCAP's training director. McGonegal's day job is as a chemist and he often speaks at cider events on topics like sensory analysis. He began with the "do's and don'ts" of judging. "Be Punctual," read the PowerPoint slide. "Be Ready. Clear Mind, Clear of Scent, Clear Palate." The judges were told to "Be Observant" and to "Describe, Don't Guess." Finally: "Be Deliberate" and "Be Kind."

After that, McGonegal took us through the judging score sheet: Bouquet/Aroma (scents categorized as Fruit, Fermented, Funk) would be scored up to ten points; Flavor/Mouthfeel (elements of Sweetness, Acidity, Bitterness, Carbonation, Astringency, Viscosity, Finish, and Other) would be scored up to 26 points; Appearance (primarily Hue and Clarity) would get four points. Then, there would be an Overall score of up to ten points (judgments such as Classic/Not to Style; Flawless/Significant Flaws; Wonderful/Lifeless). Fifty points would be a perfect score. "Appearance used to get six points," McGonegal said. "Now it gets four points. We moved those two points to mouthfeel. Also, don't judge for carbonation. Some people have gotten hung up on it. I'm asking you, please don't."

Working in groups of two or three judges, we were supposed to come to a consensus score—if we all differed by more than 3 points, at least one of us would have to change our score. Once we'd debated and discussed this consensus, we'd then award a medal—Gold (45 points and above), Silver (38 to 44 points), or Bronze (30 to 37 points)—or, in rare cases, no medal at all. The majority of ciders would win some type of medal, we were told. We were given sample score sheets and a stapled, 19-page document of GLINTCAP judging criteria for each of the various categories.

McGonegal discussed a number of flaws that we should look out for: vinegary or sulfur smells, volatile acidity, oxidation, aromas similar to nail polish remover, and ciders that had what he called "elbows." Someone raised their hand. "Charles, you've used a word, *elbows*, that I'm not familiar with."

"He means awkward!" someone else shouted from across the ballroom.

I was a bit surprised by the focus on flaws. I realized that about 20 percent of GLINTCAP's entries would be from amateurs, but it was hard to believe a commercial cidery would release ciders with such obvious problems.

No flaw was more of a cardinal sin for McGonegal than ciders that exhibited "mouse" taint. "If a cider is mousy, it does not get a medal," he said. I'd heard a lot about mouse in discussions over natural wines—mostly from people who do not like natural wines. There's not been much study on mousiness, but it's believed to be lactic bacteria triggered by too-aggressive Brettanomyces yeast. A little Brettanomyces can add complexity to fermented beverages, while too much of it causes a sort of barnyard or sweaty horse blanket aroma. Mousiness, however, is a different issue—it seems to be activated by saliva and lingers on the palate like dog breath. I don't believe it's as common as detractors of natural wine like to assert. And it's certainly not the same thing as the attractive funky aromas in many beverages.

McGonegal took a hard line on mouse. "Hopefully, we'll have someone who's mouse-sensitive in every group. We don't like mousy ciders to sneak through." Not everyone can detect mouse; up to a third of humans cannot. So we were told there would be water mixed with baking soda available during the judging and that if we suspected mouse, we should swish it in our mouths to raise the pH level—making it easier to detect the flaw—and taste again. McGonegal insisted that anyone who didn't understand mousiness should stay after class to smell a flawed cider that he had with him.

After McGonegal's presentation, we were put through a few trial tastings. The first trial was a sample entry in the "Heritage Dry" category—this was the first year that this new category would be judged at GLINTCAP. We tasted the cider and the people at my table agreed that it was fine: nothing special, nothing offensive. For me, the cider did not meet the overall criteria for Heritage Dry in the 19-page stapled document we'd received, which was "a refreshing drink of some substance." At my table, we debated this for a few minutes. I wanted to award a bronze, but in the end I gave in to the majority, and we awarded a silver.

McGonegal took a poll of the room, most of the other tables also gave this Heritage Dry a silver medal—except for one that gave it a bronze. He asked the table that had given a bronze to defend its low score. I realized that everyone sitting at this particular table was from New England, and they insisted that this cider did not have the acidity, tannins, or complexity to be Heritage Dry. They further insisted that it was miscategorized and should have been judged as a Modern Dry. McGonegal pushed back on their assessment. "The chemist in me says there's no difference between heritage and modern, in my humble opinion," he said.

I raised my hand, and reminded McGonegal that the United States Association of Cider Makers, in their brand-new Style Guide, described heritage cider as having "increased complexity" and "complex aromatics." I was aware that GLINTCAP used different criteria in its judging, but after hearing about the USACM's style guidelines for months, I figured I'd raise that point. McGonegal dismissed me by saying, "Well, as a chemist, I've never been able to test for complexity."

The tasting trial continued with a modern semi-dry that some judges felt was miscategorized. "This is a sweet cider and it shouldn't be judged against the semi-dry ciders," someone said. Then we got to the fruit cider category and were given a sample of an apricot cider. For me, the apricot cider was pretty much an average example of its type, and my table agreed. We gave it a bronze. But one judge was so irked by the apricot cider that he stood and insisted it deserved no medals at all. "There's no apricot taste!" he said. "If it doesn't taste like apricot, it can't win a medal!"

"What did this cider get last year?" McGonegal asked the other GLINTCAP volunteers.

"It got gold!" one of them shouted from the back. "It got a gold medal!"

When the session finally ended, I felt even more confounded than I did before the judges' training. There had been so much dispute in the room, so much discrepancy between medals and opinions—and the actual competition did not even begin until the following day. Also, how could one of the people running this competition be so dismissive of the obvious differences between heritage and modern ciders or about the concept of complexity in beverages?

Later that night, I returned to the same bar where I'd been the night before with a group of cider makers. It was karaoke night again, and the same guy who had channeled Axl Rose the night before was now singing Alice in Chains. Ryan Burk, from Angry Orchard, was one of the cider makers in the group. Over a badly sung rendition of "Man in the Box," I told him some of the highlights from the training session. "Some people just suck the soul out of cider," he said.

* * *

At breakfast in the same ballroom the following morning, we were given a pep talk by a guy named Rex Halfpenny, the publisher of Michigan Beer Guide, and GLINTCAP's Judge Captain. "You're going to taste about 1,400 alcoholic beverages over the next couple days," Halfpenny said. "You need to taste with a sense of urgency. No cruising." We would be tasting ciders from all over the US, as well as Canada, France, Spain, England, and even Estonia and Australia.

But we would be tasting everything blind and so we'd only know the ciders by category, number, and a brief description. Halfpenny suggested that there might be a perfect 50 lurking in today's entries. "In theory. I've never seen one. But maybe today?" He asked us to be fair and kind. "Maybe it's a 37 or 38, between a bronze and silver. You have the power to choose. But give the guy a break and kick him up."

A lot of cider makers were clearly given a break over the next two days. Out of 1,334 ciders entered in GLINTCAP, medals would be awarded to 1,177 of them—meaning that if you simply paid the $60 fee to enter a cider, you had an 88 percent chance of winning a medal. I realize that this information may undercut whatever competitive drama GLINTCAP promised. But honestly, even though I personally blind-tasted at least a hundred ciders across numerous categories, my role as a judge felt like an exercise in futility.

There seemed to be an inordinate, almost comical, focus on discerning flaws. I was assigned to the Fruit Cider category on the first day. My fellow judge, from Indiana, and I were mostly in agreement on a handful of laughably bad ciders in our flight—a circus of Meyer lemons, raspberries, and pomegranates. The last cider we tasted was co-fermented with tart cherries. It was a disaster, an utterly terrible cider that didn't deserve any kind of medal. I was ready to compromise and give it a bronze and move on with my day, but my fellow judge kept sniffing and sipping. Finally he raised the dreaded issue of mousiness. "Are you sensitive to mouse?" he asked.

"Yeah, I'm pretty sure," I said. "But I don't detect mouse here."

"Did you stay after at the training last night with Charles?" he asked. I told him no, that I'd instead gone to a karaoke bar. He said: "I think we'd better go get the baking soda to make our mouths more alkaline." He waved to Rex Halfpenny, who brought us the baking soda water. We swished and gargled and tasted again. It still didn't taste mousy. But it still definitely tasted like a bad cider.

"I don't know," I said.

"Are you sure you're sensitive to mouse?" he asked.

Finally, we summoned McGonegal, who happened to be sitting a few tables away. "Charles, do you get mouse here?" McGonegal strolled over to us with an air of majesty. He took the terrible tart cherry cider, swigged and looked up toward the ceiling as he swished the cider in his mouth. As he swished, I said, "If it's mousy, it's only very slightly."

At that exact moment, McGonegal spat, and declared, "Yes. Mousy." Then, pointing to me, he added: "But like he said, only slightly." It was as if I'd performed the old Jedi mind trick—*These aren't the droids you are looking for.*

Most of my time as a judge during GLINTCAP was spent on the "Heritage Cider—Dry" category. It was these rounds of judging that were the most disheartening. To begin with, roughly half the ciders I judged in this category were actually semi-dry and not dry. But it was more than that.

The very first dry heritage cider of the competition that I judged was described in the notes as "Asturian"—though I didn't know whether it was actually from Spain or an American cider made in that style. I gave the "Asturian" cider a solid silver-medal score, but one of my fellow judges, a nice guy from Michigan, immediately disagreed. "I smell acetone," he said, referring to the aroma reminiscent of nail polish remover. I did not discern nail polish remover at all.

"Do you mean acetified?" I asked, clarifying the vinegar-like aroma of acetic acid that's often present in Spanish ciders when they're inert—the reason for the traditional aerating long pour.

"No," he insisted, "I think this cider is flawed. Or at least it's miscategorized." He thought it should have been entered in the "Natural Cider" category. I didn't agree, but since we had to arrive at a consensus score, that cider received a bronze medal.

In a subsequent round, also "Heritage Cider—Dry," another of my fellow judges dismissed a couple of lovely, potentially gold-medal-scoring ciders. "All I smell is acetone," he said. These were not Spanish ciders. They were American ciders blended with wild crab apples. Acetone seemed to have become a catchall term for strange aromas that certain people didn't like.

"I don't know," I said. "I don't think that's acetone. I think that's just what wild crab apples from the Northeast smell like."

I could certainly empathize with a judge from another part of the country not knowing that aroma, but it most certainly was not a flaw. Even in our 19-page stapled document of GLINTCAP guidelines, under the criteria for Heritage Cider, it clearly stated: "Dry ciders will be more wine-like with some esters." Esters, by definition, are volatile, a reaction between acid and alcohol, that create sometimes very unique aromas in fermented beverages. Esters in cider might create aromas that don't smell like apples, just as wine doesn't necessarily smell like grapes. Riesling can smell like petrol, nebbiolo can smell like tar and roses, and gewürztraminer can smell like lychee and roses. When dealing with more complex apple varieties, grown in different regions, the chances for unique aromas multiplied. Northern Spy grown in New York's Finger Lakes or Vermont's Champlain Valley could show markedly different flavors and aromas than Northern Spy grown in Michigan's Fruit Ridge or in Oregon's Willamette Valley.

I think it was during the GLINTCAP judging that I finally lost my patience with the cider community's reluctance to deal in what too many people called "pretentious wine talk." The more complex apple varieties that orchardists across America are growing for the heritage category require a more sophisticated and nuanced approach. Instead, too many of the judges at GLINTCAP acted as though they were detectives, on the hunt for flaws. It started to feel like an agenda.

On the last afternoon, I judged the semifinals of the Best in Class round for the Heritage Dry category. One of my fellow judges for this round was an amateur cider maker named Mike, from Washington State, who showed us a photo of the GLINTCAP gold medals he'd won for his homemade ciders. Before we started, I opened up the 19-page criteria document so we could all review it. Mike from Washington said, "Don't read that too literally. You don't want to be too literal."

I looked at him quizzically. "But this is the criteria for Heritage Dry," I said. "Isn't judging criteria supposed to be literal?"

For this Best in Class round, they served a dozen ciders at once—all of which had been awarded gold medals—and we had to select three to move through to the finals. We all tasted silently for a few minutes. I was the first one to speak: "I'm just putting this out there, but I think cider number 745 is fantastic."

"Ugh," said Mike from Washington. "I was just about to say I hate that one. All I get is acetone on the nose."

"That's not acetone," I said. "That's what crab apples from the northeastern United States smell like sometimes. It's a regional variation. Not a flaw."

Mike looked at me as if to say: *Who the hell let you into this judging?* "I know you're saying that the apples in your little local area taste like this, but it's a flaw."

"My little local area?" I said, with a laugh. "You mean . . . New York? The Northeast?"

In the spirit of GLINTCAP, however, we compromised. Heritage Dry cider #745—which smelled either like northeastern crab apples or acetone—was tossed aside. But we also discarded a sweet, appley one-note cider, likely made with dessert fruit, that Mike advocated for. The compromise, of course, was to send through a semi-dry cider from Virginia, which was described in the notes as being made with both wild apples and dessert apples, such as Stayman and Mutsu. This cider later won Best in Class as a "heritage dry" cider.

As I caught a taxi back to the Gerald R. Ford Airport to fly home from Grand Rapids, I was frustrated and a little angered by what clearly seemed to be a bias against true heritage cider makers, predominantly from the traditional cider regions of the Northeast, working with real cider apples and wild fruit. It reminded me a little of the antagonism that natural wines face from the wine establishment, which often harps on the supposed "flaws." But if wine is too pretentious to deal with, another close comparison we can make is the pushback that New England–style IPAs faced from the craft beer community not too long ago. Beers like Vermont's Heady Topper, that people now drive hundreds of miles to stand in line for, were excoriated at first by craft beer geeks. The New England IPAs were hazy, high alcohol, and "juicy." The craft beer establishment called them—wait for it—*flawed*. Was it any coincidence that these "flawed" beers put a dent in the dominance of classic, hoppy West Coast IPAs?

I was not surprised to learn, a few weeks after my visit to Grand Rapids, that many of the best cider makers I've spent time with—and written about in this book—did not even enter GLINTCAP. Unsurprisingly, there were zero entries from Aaron Burr. Almost none of the Finger Lakes producers participated. Not Eve's Cidery, South Hill, Redbyrd, Blackduck, or Kite & String (the only Finger Lakes producer that did, Black Diamond, won a few Best in Class awards). Few New England producers entered, with conspicuous absences by Shacksbury, Carr's Ciderhouse, Fable Farm Fermentory, and West County. I had seen LouLou Spencer in Grand Rapids as a judge, but Farnum Hill did not enter any ciders. It wasn't just the Northeast:

There were no entries from Tilted Shed, Art + Science, or Albemarle CiderWorks. Of the 105 medals won by New York ciders, Angry Orchard won 20 of them. Meanwhile, Michigan cideries won the most medals, with 134. Charles McGonegal's ÆppelTreow won two gold medals.

At CiderCon and other cider events throughout the winter there had been talk about the "big tent" of the cider community. On my way home from Grand Rapids, the big tent felt a little ripped.

CHAPTER 11
CIDER'S LEAP TOWARD IMMORTALITY

Despite my frustration with GLINTCAP, I did enjoy the morning I spent judging fortified cider and apple-based spirits. Not quite because of the entries, the overall quality of which was some of the worst I encountered at the competition—even worse than the Fruit Cider category involving the tart cherry cider that may or may not have had a hint of mouse. I enjoyed judging apple brandies and pommeau because I was paired with two of the country's finest pommeliers and cider evangelists, Ambrosia Borowski, the general manager at Chicago's premier cider bar, The Northman, and Mattie Beeson, owner of the Black Twig, a Basque-themed cider bar in Durham, North Carolina (and creator of Txotxfest). Among the more infamous entries we bonded over were an apple brandy so dangerously redolent of fusel alcohol that we worried about going blind and something we dubbed "prison pommeau" because it tasted like the sort of thing an inmate might make under the radiator in his cell.

After the competition Borowski and I began a conversation about our love of Calvados, the famed apple brandy from Normandy. Calvados begins life as cider, similar to how brandies like Cognac or Armagnac are distilled from wine. Like all brandies, Calvados can age decades and live forever in the bottle as a taste of the apple harvest. As Borowski said, "Calvados is cider's leap toward immortality." Alongside The Northman's large ever-changing cider menu, she had more than 40 Calvados on offer. Not long after GLINTCAP, I had to write a tasting report on Calvados—meaning I would have to taste and review almost 100 samples. The Northman seemed like a perfect place to do some of this tasting, and so I went to Chicago to continue the conversation.

In Chicago I'd rented an AirBnB above The Northman (touted as a "CiderBnB") that stocked complimentary Uncle John's Cider in the fridge. I didn't have to walk too many steps to go back and forth between my room and the bar. That was fortunate, since I'd spend the better part of three days inside that bar. When I wasn't tasting brandy, I was sampling The Northman's ciders. I was struck by how different the selection was here from cider lists in the Northeast. Borowski told me that her customers veered more toward semi-dry ciders. "I think most people getting into cider need a little sweetness," she said. "A little sweetness adds body and aromatics." Beyond a preference for semi-dry, there was regionality. Farnum Hill was the only northeastern producer on the menu, which was dominated by Midwestern and Western offerings such as Vander Mill and Uncle John's from Michigan, Stem Ciders from Colorado, and E.Z. Orchards and Finnriver from Oregon. It was at The Northman that I discovered fascinating ciders from 2 Towns and Wandering Aengus—Oregon producers I had not yet encountered. When I later learned that 2 Towns had won a gold medal and a dozen silver medals at GLINT-CAP, my faith was somewhat restored in the competition.

I was particularly drawn to Wandering Aengus' single-varietal Calville Blanc d'Hiver. "Calville's winter white" is an old French apple, so this cider would probably be classified as "heritage." But in France, Calville Blanc d'Hiver is the preferred choice for the classic tarte Tatin—so could one also say, technically, that this was a dessert apple. The ciders from 2 Towns on the menu were also French inspired—one called Cidre Bouché, aged in French oak casks, and another made with 100 percent Bulmers Norman, a cider apple from Normandy that jumped the Channel and became popular in the UK. This was no surprise, since Borowski considered herself an unabashed Francophile, and likely served more Normandy cider, from producers like Etienne Dupont and Christian Drouin, than any other bar in the US. Which is how The Northman ended up accumulating more Calvados on its back bar than anywhere else.

I spent my afternoons in Chicago holed up in one of The Northman's heavy, dark-wood booths, sipping and taking notes, as Borowski prepped for the evening service. She'd been to Normandy several times, as I had in my work writing about spirits, and we swapped stories about the various producers on the list. As I tasted deeper and deeper into the Calvados, I realized I was peeling back the onion on my own cider experiences. It was my research trips to Normandy, starting a decade before, where my seminal cider and apple knowledge had come from.

* * *

There are no wine appellations in Normandy. Grapes, revered elsewhere in France, are an afterthought in this region along the English Channel on France's northwest coast, about a two-hour drive from Paris. The climate is just too unpredictable—hot and sunny one moment, rainy and windy the next. Forget about grapes in Normandy. Here, the apple is king. Cider and Calvados go hand in hand.

Outside France, spirits aficionados tend to overlook Calvados when discussing the world's great brandies, the focus and attention too often on Cognac and Armagnac. But those among us who love the apple brandy from Normandy know what the uninitiated are missing. No less than the great *New Yorker* writer A. J. Liebling, in his classic food memoir *Between Meals*, declared Calvados "the best alcohol in the world." In Liebling's opinion, Calvados "has a more agreeable bouquet, a warmer touch to the heart, and more outgoing personality than Cognac." Though, he did admit that "not everybody has had the advantage of a good early soaking in the blessed liquid."

"Usually people who like Calvados like spirits with personality," said Guillaume Drouin, who runs Christian Drouin, his family's distillery. It's not an overstatement to say that after a meal, Calvados touches the heart warmly. While I've fallen in and out of lust with many spirits over the years, Calvados is my one true love that I keep returning to. Over the past decade, I've witnessed its evolution—which somewhat resembles cider's evolution in the US.

Even within France, Calvados has struggled with its reputation. Sixty years ago, there were about 15,000 Calvados producers in Normandy, most of them unlicensed. These were farmers who distilled apple brandy for personal consumption, much of it rough stuff that became known by the slang term *calva*—the sort of thing old men drank with their morning coffee. Now, just over 300 producers remain in the 2,100-square-mile region of Calvados, though only about 20 brands are known outside the region. It has taken time, but slowly over the past two decades, a serious generation of Calvados producers has elevated the spirit into the discussion about the world's great brandies. "We are a young generation making a product that's old-fashioned," Jean-Roger Groult, sixth-generation distiller at Roger Groult told me. "We're dusting off the image of Calvados." Still, great Calvados never forgets its rustic roots. Some aspects of tradition are timeless, such as the *Trou Normand*, "the Norman hole," in which Calvados is served between courses at a large meal to cleanse the palate and make room for more.

Normandy is a place of genuine multi-use farms. There is still a traditional designation of *fermier* ("farm-made") cider and Calvados. You'll see handmade signs for it as you drive along the Route du Cidre, a 25-mile loop that winds through orchards and picturesque villages with half-timbered houses—Bonnebosq, Beaufour-Druval,

Beuvron-en-Auge, and Cambremer. Pays d'Auge, the most prestigious of Calvados' three appellations, now has 59 producers, though only around 15 or so are widely known outside France. Pays d'Auge is also where some of France's most famed cheeses are made, from the towns of Camembert, Pont-l'Évêque, and Livarot. Many Calvados producers here are also dairy farmers. The best orchard sites may also be where herds of cows graze, throughout summer, under the apple trees. This is the case even in the orchards of top producers.

There's true synergy in this shared agriculture. As the fruit ripens on the trees, the cows grazing in the orchard start getting hungry for apples, and begin thumping the trunks to make them fall. When the first apples do fall, the cows devour them off the ground. "The cows are doing my job for me," Drouin once told me. "Because the first apples they make fall are overripe or diseased or somehow unusable. And once we see them begin to eat those apples, we move the cows from the orchard. That's when I know it's about time for harvest."

Making quality Calvados—to return to an old saw—begins in the orchard. Norman producers are permitted to use dozens of varieties, and some blends use 40 or more varieties. Calvados requires an extremely high percentage of bittersharp and bittersweet apple varieties, and the most prevalent have names like Antoinette, Frequin Rouge, Bisquet, Moulin à Vent, or Mettais. These bring the acidity and tannins necessary for structure and long aging. They're blended with a smaller percentage of sweet varieties like Rouge Duret or Noël des Champs along with sharps like Rambaud, Petit Jaune, or René Martin. The major reason why most American apple brandy is nowhere near as complex as Calvados—just as with cider—is because, in the US, mostly dessert apples are used.

Cider is essential to the process. "You can't make good Calvados if you don't make good cider," Drouin said. For the best producers, cider fermentation is natural and slow. "It's very important for the cider to have a long fermentation," I was told by Emmanuel Camut, who runs Adrien Camut with his brother Jean-Gabriel. "That's the only way you get a lot of complexity." Traditionally, cider rests for up to a year in old barrels before it's distilled, usually just before the new harvest. When I have visited Camut in early September, for instance, they are draining the casks of cider into their wood-fired pot stills, distilling it to make room for the new cider they will soon press after the harvest.

After the orchard, pressing, fermentation, and distillation comes the most important aspect of producing Calvados: aging. Many believe the greatest Calvados come from 30 or more years in the barrel. But to be clear, quality in Calvados is not simply a question of long aging. There is good Calvados at every age, even with just a few years in the barrel. In fact, young Calvados is much more drinkable and enjoyable than young Cognac or Armagnac. What are we looking for when we taste great Calvados? That was something Borowski and I debated throughout my time at The Northman. Guillaume Drouin once told me that great Calvados should have ambition and complexity. Others, like Emmanuel Camut or Jean-Roger Groult, will tell you that they believe Calvados should always maintain a core of beautiful rusticity. I think both are right. One critical aspect of tasting Calvados is that there should always be some note, however fleeting or haunting, of the actual apple from the orchard. In younger Calvados that might come across as ripe, crisp fruit or perhaps apple pie or strudel. But in older Calvados, the unmistakable aromas, and savory, astringent notes of the apple's peel are an indicator of quality. In this way Calvados is quite different from grape brandies like Cognac and Armagnac. "I love Armagnac," said Jean-Roger Groult. "But I never taste it or smell it and say, 'Ah, there's the grape.'"

This was what Borowski insisted was the most important element. "I always look for complexity that circles back to the apple," she said. "The aging process should enhance the fruit's complexity, not cover it up."

* * *

Tasting Calvados at The Northman called back images of meandering the narrow roads of Normandy's Route du Cidre.

Once, a young woman at the rental car desk in Paris asked me where I was heading. When I told her Normandy, she asked, "Ah, you're going to visit the D-Day beaches like the other Americans?"

"No," I said. "I'm actually going to drink Calvados."

She looked at me blankly. "Calvados? What is that?"

My meek reply: "It's, um, an apple brandy. From Normandy."

With a shrug of Parisian nonchalance, she said, "Ah, I think my grandfather used to drink this with his morning coffee."

This reaction is the kind of thing that makes Calvados distillers wince, and I got an earful from the younger generation of producers on that trip. "We want to go away from this image of the *café-calva* and move to that of a noble spirit," I was told by Jérôme Dupont, then in his early 40s, who'd taken over his family's Domaine Dupont. "A lot of people in France think cider and Calvados producers must be 70-year-old farmers, and very conservative." Even in Normandy, cider was not taken as seriously as it should. "Even locally, chefs still think cider is not good enough to be served with food," he said, exasperated. All this clearly pained Dupont, an innovator who was the first person to ever pour me a cider made in the Champagne method, with second fermentation in the bottle. He was also the first one I knew to be experimenting with bringing Belgian beer styles into cider making. With Calvados, Dupont was doing whiskey-like experiments with bottling cask-strength 30-year-old Calvados.

Dupont was part of a group called Esprit Calvados that had

formed in the late 2000s, along with Jean-Roger Groult, Christian Drouin, and several others in their 30s and 40s who'd recently taken over their family distilleries. Esprit Calvados promoted a new image of the age-old spirit and brought Calvados into the 21st century, as well as reclaiming traditional farming and distilling practices. I'd come on that trip to write about Esprit Calvados. But driving the Route du Cidre, passing half-timbered houses and orchards with cattle grazing beneath the apple trees, it felt equally important to make pilgrimages to the traditional makers of *cidre fermier*.

Along the Route du Cidre, you can't go wrong if you stop wherever there's a sign with a little apple that reads "Cru de Cambremer," designating one of 18 farms whose cider and Calvados meets a high mark of quality. There, the farmer likely has a small tasting room where you can try cider, brandy, as well as Pommeau de Normandie, a blend of Calvados and fresh-pressed juice—about as far from prison pommeau as one can get.

A little past Bonnebosq, I followed the first "Cru de Cambremer" sign that I saw, down a gravel road, past a farmhouse and up to an unadorned building, with the same dark wood exterior as the barn next door; only a small sign signified that this was the tasting room for "G & J-L Cenier." No one was around, but the door was open, so I walked inside. Bottles of cider labeled *cidre fermier* lined a small wooden bar along with the Calvados, as well as wheels of pungent local cheeses. An aging poster on the wall, showing glasses with angel wings, proclaimed, "*Le Cidre est legér, de 50 calories/verre*," making a pitch for the diet conscious.

A few moments later, Ginette Cenier, the smiling, middle-aged owner, entered the room and, without a lot of chitchat, began pouring samples of the ciders, both dry and semi-dry, as well as a poiré—all funky and delicious. She then moved onto the pommeau, followed by two Calvados, her four-year-old Vieux, and seven-year-old Hors d'Âge. While it was perhaps not as flashy as the experimental bottlings of the Esprit Calvados producers, this was good honest cider and Calvados.

"Do you export this?" I asked.

Cenier chuckled. "Only very little, and only within Europe," she said. "Not for Americans."

I visited a half-dozen quality farmer-producers like this one as I traversed the Route du Cidre—and pretty much every tasting room offered the same three styles of cider (dry, semi-dry, pear), pommeau, and two or three Calvados. Besides Cenier, my personal favorite was Manoir de Grandouet at the farm of the Grandval family. In the adorable town of Beuvron en Auge (one of the "Hundred Loveliest Villages in France") I stopped at the Relais de la Route du Cidre, where I tasted and bought some bottles from producers I couldn't visit.

When I visited Christian Drouin, a busload of noisy German tourists had just left to return to the seaside resorts of Deauville and Trouville, and in the half-timbered tasting room, I was all alone with a glass of a 1963 vintage of the world's finest apple brandy. Guillaume Drouin, who'd taken over from his father, Christian, a few years before, was pouring me vintages dating back to the mid-20th century. I'd enjoyed sipping the 1970, my birth year. The 1992 was pretty and austere, the 1986 big and floral, and the 1961 profound. But I kept circling back to the 1963, and begging Drouin for just a little more. As someone who has sampled some of the finest and rarest examples of Cognac, Armagnac, pot-still rum, single-cask bourbon, and just about everything else, I can tell you that this 1963 Christian Drouin Calvados was one of the strangest, most complex spirits I'd encountered: aromas and flavors of the forest and the bakery—butterscotch, pine, mushroom, chocolate, exotic spices—and above all, the taste of the greatest crisp apple tart. Every time I came back to the glass, there was something different, and the finish stayed with me long after the glass was empty.

"What do you think?" asked Drouin.

"I don't know if I can properly describe this," I said. "Can I say that it's both rustic and elegant at the same time?"

Drouin didn't seem surprised. "A Calvados like this is more complex than even a premier cru of Bordeaux or Burgundy," he said. "This has the same level of ambition."

He then pulled out something even rarer than the 1963, a bottle from 1939, which even predates the official appellation. Drouin's 1939 vintage is the only Calvados that's been certified from before the German occupation of the Second World War (that's mainly because whatever the Germans didn't destroy, they drank). The last bottling of this happened in 1986, after 47 years in the barrel, and there are now only a handful of bottles left in existence. Does it really matter if I tell you that the flavors and aromas here are ancient, delicate, smoky, endlessly expansive, full of rancio, and impossible to wrap one's mind around? The spirit was a time capsule.

The next morning, as I drove south toward the village of Saint-Cyr-du-Ronceray to visit Roger Groult, I passed orchard after orchard, each with cows grazing under the apple trees. Outside Saint-Cyr-du-Ronceray, I stopped at a small café, where several older men were reading newspapers and sipping coffee along with a shot of young Calvados—the classic *café et calva*. I ordered one, too, and the men watched me as I winced a bit at the spirit's roughness. One of the men laughed, held up his glass, and said, "Santé." This is precisely the image that Esprit Calvados is trying to change. And yet, deep down, this rustic tradition is part of Calvados' character.

When I arrived for a visit at Roger Groult, Jean-Roger Groult, then in his early 30s, showed off the family's traditional wood-fired stills, and century-old barrels that are never quite drained of their rootstock—the newer Calvados is always added to a cask that still has the remnants of decades-old brandy. It's a fitting metaphor for the new-wave producers. Groult poured me his oldest bottle, Doyen d'Age, a blend of brandies that is much older than he was. This Calvados was mind-bendingly complex: smoky, floral, and spiced, but still having the core aroma and flavor of gorgeous baked apple. We both stood silent for a few moments as we sniffed and sipped. It was a timeless moment and I will always remember it.

All of those memories came back to me as I tasted the Calvados that afternoon at The Northman. It also all came back to me—the land, the tradition, the people—when I drank the Norman cider from Domaine Dupont on tap later with dinner at the bar. This feeling is something that's not talked about enough in the world of cider, how a sip can transport you through time and place. We talk about this all the time with wine and spirits, but it can also happen with cider. At least certain styles of cider.

That summer, as I was preparing for another research trip to Calvados, I learned that Jérôme Dupont of Domaine Dupont, had died prematurely, at the age of 48. Guillaume Drouin emailed me the horrible news a few days before I was to leave for France. Jérôme's tragic death is profoundly felt within the tight-knit circle of Pays d'Auge producers. He was such a tireless advocate of cider and Calvados, traveling around the world to share his enthusiasm. Certainly the future direction of Domaine Dupont is now unclear.

Personally, the news affected me because Jérôme was exactly my age, and I admired him greatly. But more than that, I think this is a reminder that when we talk about artisan producers, we're talking about specific people and families, who make with their own hands these products we drink. It's not all just a romantic story; there is always struggle. Life is hard, as people who live near the beaches of

Normandy know as well as anyone. I believe both cider and Calvados embody this humanity and truth.

As I traveled around Calvados, I stopped one day for lunch in Pont l'Évêque at a place I like called Restaurant Le Saint-Mélaine Bouchon Normand. On the chalkboard, alongside authentic dishes like calves head, poisson du jour á la Normande, and classic tarte Tatin, a cider special was listed: Domaine Dupont Cidre Réserve by the bottle. This was one of Jérôme's innovations, aged six months in a Calvados barrel.

I ordered the Dupont Cidre Réserve with the plat du jour, and the server popped it open and poured it into my glass. This cider was fragrant and a bit funky at first, but then elegant and full of spice. In the mouth it was semi-dry, with significant residual sugar—the way most cider in Normandy is made. I'd become so accustomed to dry cider that the element of sweetness came like a punch, but it undoubtedly added complexity to the dense, powerful fruit flavors and tannins. I silently toasted Jérôme as I drank his cider. I thought about the Calvados that would come from Domaine Dupont over the coming decades, made from cider just like this. Even 30 or 40 years from now, when I am hopefully nearing 80 or 90, I will still be able to taste apple brandy that Jérôme himself brought from the orchard, through fermentation and distillation, and stored in a barrel. Perhaps that's as close to immortality as one can hope for in this earthly life.

CHAPTER 12

SELLING THE REVIVAL

The American cider region most closely resembling Normandy's Route du Cidre exists on the isthmus between Seneca and Cayuga Lakes in New York. So as spring blossomed, I returned, yet again, to the Finger Lakes.

One hot afternoon, I made another visit to Eric Shatt's Redbyrd Orchard at his home near Trumansburg, where he was grafting scion to rootstock to propagate new trees. "This is really our first warm day," he said. "It's a late spring season." In the back of his pickup truck, he had stacks of the scion, or budwood, that he'd taken from some of his 2,000 apple trees. "I sold a lot of budwood this winter," he said. "It was a good side business."

Shatt was doing what's called cleft grafting. With his knife, he cut an incision into a thick branch of a four-year-old tree. Then he took a long, thin twig with new buds, shaved the end, and fit it snugly into the cleft in the rootstock. "If this takes, it will probably start growing in a couple of weeks," he said. "The tree doesn't need a lot of contact to graft. Even with a dull knife like mine."

After the budwood was snug in the rootstock, Shatt carefully wrapped the incision and coated it in a yellow goo called Doc Farwell's Grafting Seal.

"What's that?" I asked.

"I don't know," he said, with a chuckle. "Egg yolks? It looks like Grey Poupon." Then, like a surgeon, he quickly moved on to the next graft.

The scion wood that Shatt was grafting had come from another wild apple variety he'd discovered. "This is my new favorite. I call it Redbyrd Bitter. I found the seedling by the cidery." He already had 40 trees of Redbyrd Bitter and wanted to add more.

The Redbyrd Bitter's circle of life is fascinating: Shatt had grafted the original to rootstock seven years before and propagated the trees. Then, in the summer of 2016, he cut budwood from those trees and gave them to a local nursery to grow more on a larger scale. By the following year, the nursery had grown a bunch of new young trees, and they pulled them out and sold them back to Redbyrd. The nursery would also sell young Redbyrd Bitter trees to other orchardists. "I'm so glad I did this, because the mother tree is now dead," Shatt said. "It's supercool that it could become a variety that makes good cider for a lot of people."

I asked Shatt what he looked for in a wild apple. "Flavor, of course," he said. "Lately I've also been including size into the parameters I take into account. It's so much work to pick small apples. And the small ones can gum up the press." But just as important is the wild apple's disease and drought resistance—and the fact that it has been a winner in the Darwinian game of natural selection. "That's an advantage with wild apples," he said. "They've obviously survived years in the wild. They're hardy."

As if to underscore the point, he walked me down a row of what once had been trees of the Medaille d'Or variety. Medaille d'Or is a French bittersweet variety, grown from a seedling in 19th-century Normandy, along the Seine river. It's a classic cider variety, but here in the Finger Lakes, they fell victim to the black stem borer, a pesty beetle. "We lost them all," Shatt said. "This is becoming an emerging problem." The beetles are attracted to the ethylene produced by young, immature trees. They then lay their eggs and infect the trees with a fungus that eventually kills the tree. "The beetles are seeking out the weakest trees," he said. So the black stem borer can be added to the list of other orchard problems for cider apples.

Shatt took a break from grafting, and we tasted his Cloudsplitter, the cider I'd watched him press seven months before. Dark golden, almost amber, it had big tannins and thrilling, sauvignon blanc–like acidity at the midpalate. Cloudsplitter was earthy but warm, with notes of orange blossom and honey, and a finish of grilled lemon. It's a blend of 30 varieties of apples that he changes from year to year: It included heirlooms like Golden Russet, Baldwin, Newton Pippin, crabs like Wickson and Dolgo, classic British varieties like Kingston Black, Dabinett, and Porter's Perfection, and also contained a good portion of Shatt's own varieties, Redbyrd Bitter and Gnarled Chapman. The perennial tweaking and experimentation had a purpose, Shatt insisted. "If cider continues to be produced in this way for 100 years, it will become clear which, say, five varieties will make awesome cider in the Finger Lakes," he said. "Any of these varieties could become mainstream and improve the cider of New York, or the United States in general."

For that to happen, it will take the help of specialty nurseries, where cider makers buy fruit trees—such as Fedco in Maine, run by John Bunker. In the Finger Lakes, an important tree supplier is Cummins Nursery, ten minutes down Trumansburg Road, on the outskirts of Ithaca. I visited Cummins Nursery in late spring, just as the last of the year's trees and rootstocks were about to be shipped or picked up. I arrived straight from visiting an orchard, dressed in boots, cap, and flannel, and when I met Alan Leonard, the senior nurseryman, he said, "Are you the journalist? You look like a farmer."

Cummins Nursery grows about 40,000 fruit trees per year, mostly for cider makers and hobbyists. "Let's say we do more European bittersharps and bittersweets than Honeycrisps," said Leonard. The nursery was founded by Dr. Jim Cummins, a retired Cornell professor of pomology, in the mid-1990s. According to Leonard, Dr. Cummins was a lifelong teetotaler who only developed a taste for cider when he was in his early 90s. Cummins works closely with the Finger Lakes cider community. The nursery helped propagate Shatt's Redbyrd Bitter and Gnarled Chapman. Though the New York heirloom Golden Russet is still the bestseller around here—Leonard said numerous producers have told him it's the "ideal base" for good cider blends.

"Cider apples are a profound amount of work," Leonard said. "There just are not many established cider orchards." Yet since Leonard began working at Cummins in 2004, he's seen the demand for cider-variety trees quadruple. "In the past decade, it's gone crazy. The demand is always more than we can supply." But he added: "There's concern in the industry that there's a bit of a bubble."

We wandered the nursery warehouse, with wooden boxes holding trees tightly wrapped with fluorescent ties, the remaining orders for the year. Cummins Nursery gets orders for cider-apple trees from all over the country, and it has specific links on its website "For the North" and "For the South." For the South, they recommend apples like Arkansas Black or Gravenstein over many of the popular English or French cider varieties. "The Finger Lakes is a great region to grow the English and French varieties," Leonard said. "But in the South, fire blight is brutal on them. A lot of those varieties don't do well in the heat of summer." But a lot of the newcomers to cider and orchards still order the buzzword English and French varieties, such as Dabinett, Kingston Black, or Calville Blanc, anyway.

"We try to dissuade them," said Tino Navarra, Leonard's fellow nurseryman.

I asked Leonard and Navarra if they saw a certain type of person getting into the cider business. "One of the classic types is someone in their early 50s, who's retiring early and wants to start a late-career business," Leonard said. "They have no horticultural experience, but they've read somewhere that cider is going to be the next craft beer."

Beyond choosing apple varieties that may not work in other regions, another industry problem is what Navarra called "the patience factor." Many beginning orchardists opt to buy and plant smaller, so-called dwarf trees, rather than standard-sized trees, because the smaller trees will produce more fruit faster. "That's certainly appealing," Navarra said. "But dwarf trees are vastly more expensive per acre than standard trees."

The high price point of artisan cider, in general, seemed to be something that concerned both Leonard and Navarra. "Cider in Europe is a cheap drink," Navarra said, noting that most artisan cider in the US sold for around $15 per bottle or higher.

"You've met all the Finger Lakes cider makers," Leonard told me. "None of them are making much money. Even though their bottle prices are high." He seemed worried that the average drinks consumers wouldn't value a higher-priced cider in the way they do with wine. Despite their concerns, both Leonard and Navarra made clear that they believed the quality of cider justified those prices. "For apple growing," Navarra said, "it just doesn't get much better than the Finger Lakes."

Not just apples, but also pear growing, according to John Reynolds, whom I met at Blackduck Cidery in nearby Ovid the next day. At first, I didn't recognize Reynolds, because he'd trimmed his beard so that it was just stubble. "It's a summertime thing," he said. He'd also cut his long hair into a rat tail in the back, leading us both to reminisce about having rat tails in middle school in the 1980s. "I'm trying to bring it back," he said. When I arrived, Reynolds was also doing his late spring cleft grafting. Several of his farm cats were rubbing up against the grafted trees as he worked. "Yeah, the cats aren't very helpful with grafting," he said.

Reynolds was also grafting scion wood he'd taken from wild seedlings, but these were from pear trees he'd discovered while foraging in the National Forest. "The wild pears are more fire blight resistant," he said. "They've stood the test of time. A 30- to 40-year-old tree is less susceptible to disease and other problems." He planned to graft 200 trees on that day, mostly two wild varieties: one he called a Cheese Pear, with really high tannins, and another he called a Lemon Pear. "It's high acid and looks like a lemon," he said with a shrug. Over the next few days, he'd also graft scion wood of two old English perry pear varieties, Green Horse and Old Field, that he'd received from the USDA's pear repository at Oregon State University. He'd also received some budwood of varieties that originated in the Caucasus. "I'm interested in the Caucasus ones because they are completely fire blight resistant, and they're really high in tannin."

He took a break, and we tasted samples of this year's wild perry from his tanks. Reynolds told me that the reason he was experimenting with all these new pear varieties, both wild and foreign, was because he could see that his cider business was eventually going to have to change and adapt in the coming years. "At some point," he said, "I don't want to do the wild foraging anymore. It's not very efficient." The continued focus on pears, too, was part of looking forward. There had been a steady demand for Blackduck's pear ciders and blends, and it seemed like a solid niche, a way to differentiate himself in the market. Reynolds said he saw his fruit production eventually moving close to 40 percent pears and 60 percent apples.

His orchard surrounding the cidery was still young. He told me that they'd gotten 50 bushels in 2017, and planned to get 100 bushels in 2018. In two more years, they would harvest at least 700 to 800 bushels. "And when this is fully going, in say, six or seven years, then we will have to make a serious decision," he said. "If we do produce all that volume, we'd have to change how we produce and sell. Maybe we'll have to package differently. Maybe we'll can something? Maybe kegs?"

I was a little surprised to hear Reynolds talk so much about business strategy. Had shaving off the beard also shorn off a little of his rebelliousness? Then, we tasted his Spi Vs. Spy Cider, a blend of Northern Spy with Spigold apples, fruity, with balanced acidity and minerality. "This is actually my least favorite cider," he said. "I confess that sometimes I'd rather drink a beer than this." He told me about how he'd poured this cider—also informing customers it was his "least favorite cider"—during New York City Cider Week at Astor Wines & Spirits in the East Village. A store manager overheard him, and said, "But this is the cider we bought from you to sell!"

"I guess that's the last time I'll ever go to New York City Cider Week," he said.

* * *

Business strategy seemed to be on everyone's mind as summer heated up. Now that fall harvest, pressing and fermentation, winter pruning, bottling, and spring grafting were all behind them, summer actually felt like the end of the cider year. This seemed to be a time when cider makers were able to turn their attention to how to sell it.

The prior summer, the United States Association of Cider Makers had launched a social media and marketing campaign called #pickcider, targeting the Fourth of July as a holiday to be enjoyed with all-American cider. The USACM reported that the Fourth of July sales bump in 2017 was they best they'd ever seen. The #pickcider campaign seemed to be in response to concerns that had been expressed to me by cider makers like Melissa Madden at Kite & String—who bemoaned that most consumers only thought of cider during the fall.

Even iconoclastic, antiestablishment Andy Brennan of Aaron Burr was out pounding the pavement. One steaming summer afternoon, I joined him in his old Brooklyn neighborhood of Clinton Hill, and I tagged along on some sales calls. I hadn't seen Brennan for about six months. He'd skipped both CiderCon and the meeting of the New York Cider Association, even though he'd been an original member of the latter. Instead, he published an essay in *Malus* called "Cider Cons" in which he ranted about the mingling between Big Cider and smaller producers.

> I liked it better when customers were clear on their choices. Just a few years ago, they could choose a cider that was obviously from a mom-and-pop producer, or they could pick one that was clearly built from the power-of-scale production. Now mom-and-pops are incorporating "removed-from-the-land" practices, producing greater and greater volumes, while Big Cider is doing something in reverse: it's trying to appear farm-based or artisanal. Was this hybrid approach to running a cider business the consequence of the all-inclusive trade associations? Was it intentionally fostered? And at what cost are its benefits?

On this sweltering afternoon, Brennan wore a big herringbone blazer that looked like the kind of jacket a maître d' might give you when you're underdressed at a fancy restaurant. Shepherding Brennan through the sales calls was a rep from his distributor, T Edward Wines. "I'm the cider guy. For better or for worse," said the rep.

We went to Heritage Wines, a shop focusing on biodynamic, cool-climate, high-elevation, and low-intervention wines. There was a DJ's turntable on the front counter. So yes, this was clearly the proverbial hipster-Brooklyn natural wine store. When we arrived, the store manager was dealing with a shady-looking guy with a broom who claimed he was owed money because he'd swept the sidewalk in the front. The distributor's rep lined up the Aaron Burr ciders: Neversink Highlands, Summitville, Central Sullivan, Shawangunk Ridge. We all stood quietly as the manager tasted. The rep tried to prompt Brennan: "So Andy, would you say the Summitville is the most tannic?"

"Maybe," Brennan said.

"So these are all wild apples?" asked the manager.

"Well," Brennan said, "these apples are more feral than wild. Of course, after so many years, something feral becomes wild."

The manager seemed perplexed, but he liked the ciders. We chatted about mineral-driven Neversink Highlands and the funky, high-acid Shawangunk Ridge. He told Brennan that he liked the name, though he wasn't sure how people who liked *Hamilton* would react.

"We're not celebrating a murder," Brennan said. "That was the period of American history when cider culture was the strongest."

"Yeah," the manager said. "Didn't they like literally bring seeds over on the *Mayflower*?" Well, the seeds actually came a few years later, but I didn't correct him.

As we continued to taste, Brennan told us all that David Byrne had offered him apples from his property in the Catskills.

"That's cool," said the rep and the manager.

I wasn't exactly certain what sort of negotiation I was observing, but since Heritage Wines would eventually order a few bottles of Aaron Burr to stock, I figured that this sort of too-cool-for-commerce banter was just how beverage transactions in Brooklyn happened.

After the sales calls were over, Brennan, the rep, and I met Dan Pucci at a bar called Spuyten Duyvil (named after the body of water that separates the northern tip of Manhattan from the Bronx where it meets the Hudson River, called "the devil's whirlpool" by the original 17th-century Dutch settlers). Spuyten Duyvil was pouring Aaron Burr ciders, along with the other cider they had on the menu, Blackduck's Crabby Pip. Brennan ordered a magnum of his Sullivan County bottling. "So this is your cuvée?" asked Spuyten Duyvil's general manager.

"Uhhhhh," Brennan said. "I think you've thrown me. What do you mean by that?"

A few weeks later, in Washington, I joined Sam Fitz of Anxo for a staff training at a restaurant called Maydan, perhaps the hottest opening in the District of Columbia in the summer of 2018 (selected one of the best new restaurants by both *Bon Appétit* and *Food & Wine*). Maydan focuses on North African and Middle Eastern dishes (lots of harissa, chermoula, *tahina*, and *zhough*) and the room is centered around a huge open firepit where goat, lamb, and vegetables are grilled. Anxo and Maydan had collaborated on a proprietary cider for the restaurant, made from a blend of Gold Rush and Albemarle (or Newtown) Pippin from Virginia. The general manager, Said Haddad, told his staff, "This is to be served as a wine. This is not your basic carbonated Woodchuck cider. I want you guys to own this. Anxo basically made a wine just for us."

Haddad later told me, "In a lot of places a cider like this would be a tough sell. But we have natural wines, orange wines on the menu. So our guests are totally open to this."

It was exciting for me to see cider beginning to push its way onto serious wine menus and into trendy wine shops. So exciting, in fact, that I finally decided to take the exam to become a Certified Cider Professional—to formalize, I guess, the fact that my life had been completely consumed by cider. I paid my $75 one afternoon, and took the test online. Since I'd paid attention and took notes at the seminar at CiderCon in Baltimore, the questions were pretty straightforward. You had an hour to finish the exam. I took a 20-minute work phone call in the middle of it, but I still passed. I got a digital certificate to print and then a card in the mail from the executive director of the USACM—along with a CCP patch that one might sew onto an item of clothing, perhaps like an acid-washed jean jacket from the 1980s.

I was feeling pretty good about becoming a CCP. Even though I'd spent years covering wine and spirits, I'd never bothered to get any of the sommelier or mixology certifications. With cider, though, I felt like part of a select club. Soon, I would begin studying for the USACM's second level exam, to become a Certified Pommelier.

Then, I received an email press release from the USACM with a subject line that read: "Certified Cider Professional Program Gains Big with Angry Orchard Graduating Class." Apparently, nearly 500 employees from Angry Orchard had passed the CCP exam, including 400 of them in one week—doubling the number of CCPs in one fell swoop. Ryan Burk, Angry Orchard's cider maker and a USACM board member, was quoted as saying: "Angry Orchard is committed to raising awareness of cider and helping grow the industry for all cider makers. Despite the recent growth of cider in the US, the category is still small and relatively unknown, and the CCP program is a huge step towards improving awareness and education."

According to the press release, Angry Orchard's employees celebrated by "toasting with a special cider created by Burk just for the occasion." That cider—called You Down With CCP?—was reportedly "a dry unfiltered heritage cider heavy on bittersweet funk and balanced with acidity from Gold Rush and Golden Russet apples." After I read that press release, I'll admit that my own CCP certificate and patch began to feel a little less special. Now, about half of the existing CCPs worked for Angry Orchard.

In the months since the news of Angry Orchard doubling the number of CCPs, I thought a lot about Burk's assertion that, despite cider's growth, "the category is still small and relatively unknown." That was certainly true. But did it matter? Or maybe, more precisely, to whom did it matter? I'm sure size matters to Angry Orchard and to other Big Cider producers and to the ambitious start-up cideries like Shacksbury that want to grow into some type of hybrid that straddles both mass-market and heritage. But does the overall size of the category matter to crazy cider makers like Andy Brennan or John Reynolds? Does it matter to the people who grow amazing fruit from special orchards? Most of all, does it matter to drinkers who'd discovered the pleasure of drinking cider from small, artisan producers? Surely, I hope that these smaller cider makers and orchardists survive and thrive and turn some sort of a profit. And I certainly hope their ciders are available to people who have yet to discover them. But I am worried about cider growing too fast. As Dan Pucci had once said, in *Malus*: "Trees do not bend to quarterly sale forecasting, so why should cider?"

* * *

During the dog days of summer, I visited Eve's Cidery once again. Autumn was working at the winery on that day, still on her sabbatical, and I met up with her husband, Ezra Sherman, who'd taken over the day-to-day in her absence. Sherman told me that he was feeling much better than when I'd seen him the previous fall. Over the winter and spring, he'd slowly healed his ulcerative colitis, naturally and simply through diet.

As we wandered through the cidery, their son Zuri kept sneaking around behind us, hiding among tanks and boxes, and occasionally popping out to surprise us. Leila, their daughter, came home from a swimming hole with a friend and we all decided to drive up to the Albee Hill orchard. Sherman cinched the front fender of his rusted, beat-up car with rope and the kids all hopped, barefoot, onto the car roof. We puttered up the hill as the dog ran along side us. At one point, we passed a tree teeming with bright berries. I wondered what type of berries they were, so Sherman shouted up to the kids on the roof. "They're honeysuckle," Layla said, down through the sunroof. "They're poisonous."

"Nu-uh," Zuri said. "They're autumn olives. You can eat autumn olives."

"You can eat autumn olives?" Sherman said.

We arrived at the top of Albee Hill and everyone picked some ripe raspberries and blueberries on our way to the apple trees. Sherman pointed out the rows of the Frequin Rouge, a French variety that's yellow with red stripes which was becoming more important in Eve's blends. "Freakin' Rouge?" he said. "I don't know if I'm pronouncing that right." I didn't know either and we both laughed. They were still a month or more away from harvest, as was the large green Bramley's Seedling, a classic British cooking apple, that Zuri plucked from the tree.

"How does that taste?" I asked.

"Tannic," he said, and took another bite.

The kids all walked back down to the house through the woods while we returned by car. Sherman told me that running the whole orchard and cidery had been overwhelming. On any given day, he might be dealing with a tree-killing pest, renting a refrigerated truck one Friday because their cooler couldn't handle how many Champagne-method bottles needed to be disgorged, or running down to New York City to meet with their distributor. Prior to working in the cidery, he'd worked in criminal law, on both sides, for fifteen years. "I used to imagine being really good at one thing," he said. "Now, I'm back to around a four out of ten." This was clearly not true. Sherman had been working with Autumn for many years, and the cider we tasted later—single-varietal examples of Kingston Black and Frequin Rouge (Freakin' Rouge)—was delicious.

Down next to the farmhouse, Sherman showed me what they called the Valley Orchard. He pointed out trees that Angry Orchard had given them to plant. "They were giving out trees to farmers all over the Northeast," he said. "So they offered them to us, and we said, sure."

"Were there any strings attached?" I asked.

"I don't know," he said. "I don't think so?"

"Have you ever watched *The Godfather*?" I asked.

Months later, long after the harvest and pressing, after Autumn had finally returned from her sabbatical, she and I exchanged text messages. We were discussing a panel we'd proposed for CiderCon that did not get selected. In our back-and-forth, I expressed my worries about the trend toward what Andy Brennan called a "hybrid" business model: Big Cider adopting the terminology of heritage or orchard-based cider. But, for the moment, Big Cider will be limited by the apples. Right now, there just aren't enough true cider apples in America for that sort of scale. Which is why—for now—producers like Angry Orchard have focused on collaborations with highly regarded small producers. I asked Autumn what she thought of these collaborations.

"Funny you should say that," she texted. "Here's a text message I got from Ryan Burk: "Hey. Long time no see. Hope you're well and harvest is going great? Thinking . . . up to do a collab with me in the coming year? Obviously requires a conversation . . . just wanted to see if you might be interested. . . .'"

"Please don't!" I texted back. At this stage of my cider journey, the idea of Autumn collaborating with Angry Orchard caused a visceral reaction inside me. I honestly could not bear to see this happen.

After several laughing emojis, she replied: "My level of frustration with the co-option of authentic terms into meaningless marketing gunk is one of the reasons I took a sabbatical."

I asked what her response to Burk was. She texted: "Sure Ryan, when hell freezes over." Then: "No actually, I didn't. It's the only thing that came to mind to say. So I just haven't responded."

* * *

As I was nearing the end of this book in the fall of 2018, I visited once again with Andy Brennan. We were supposed to forage apples, but when I arrived Brennan told me that most of his foraging locations faced a severe lack of fruit. "This is a really off year," he said. "We have about five percent of the fruit we normally have."

"Are you worried?" I asked.

"No," he said. "Not at all. This is natural." This was the result of the dreaded biennalism, which particularly affects wild trees. Brennan said he prepares for this by picking like crazy in good years. He made lots of his Mamakating Hollow Homestead Locational Cider the prior year, for instance. "But we won't make it again for another three to four years." He drove me to a farm that had dozens of wild pippin trees he normally picks—"a pippin forest" he called it. Not one tree had fruit.

Despite the lack of apples, this year was a bumper crop for pears. And so we drove over to Mountain Side Farm, on a ridge on the border between the Catskills and the Hudson Valley. We drove up a dirt road and pulled next to two enormous trees. "This is Bert and Ernie," Brennan said. "The pear tree is Bert. And the apple tree is Ernie. Ernie gets these almost purple apples when it fruits." But Ernie had no apples this year, and so we would pick Bert, which was teeming with what Brennan called Choke Pears—"Because when you bite into them you want to choke," he said.

We began by picking the ones that had fallen on the ground. Then Brennan took a scythe and cleared out a bunch of the underbrush—there was so much poison ivy, I nearly had a panic attack, so I was no help with the scything. We laid out tarps and then took turns shaking the branches, as dozens of tiny pears rained down on to the tarps. While I shook the tree, the farmer rode up on an ATV. "Whatever you leave on the ground will be gone by morning," he said.

"I like to leave a few for the deer," Brennan said. "They're going to be doing the work of spreading the seedlings." He told the story of another farm nearby, where he'd asked if he could pick apples. That farmer wouldn't allow him. "He told me he wants the apples so the deer come, to shoot them," Brennan said. "I told him, 'I'll trade you cider!' But he said, 'I like the venison better.'"

We worked for a couple of hours. In the end, we picked two and a half bushels of choke pears. Brennan said it would make a little over six gallons of cider, about four cases of 500-milliliter bottles. It seemed like a lot of work for such a small amount of cider. I told him about Blackduck's Three Bears cider, which was a blend of pears, apples, and quince—and I wondered if maybe a blend of pears and apples might be interesting this year. About a month later, I saw Brennan at Cider Days in Massachusetts. "I took your inspiration and I've made a blend of the pears and apples," he said.

"What are you going to call it?" I asked.

"Poison Ivy, of course," he said.

* * *

On my last trip to the Finger Lakes in the fall of 2018, I went with Steve Selin to visit Stone Fence Farm, his premier apple source, from which he produces a single-orchard blend. Stone Fence Farm, near Trumansburg, is owned by 80-year-old Peter Hoover, who is revered in the bluegrass and old-time music world because of field recordings he made of traditional banjo and fiddle players in the Appalachians. After flunking out of Harvard in 1959, Hoover traveled around Tennessee, Kentucky, North Carolina, and West Virginia to sit in the living rooms of old local fiddlers and banjo pickers, and captured their music on a reel-to-reel recorder. He made more than 50 recordings that are saved at the Library of Congress and other traditional music archives, and he is credited with single-handedly preserving the sounds of a dying American tradition.

On a cold wet afternoon, Selin and I met Hoover, who had a long white, Amish-like beard, and a big green face tattooed on the back of his bald head. Hoover uses a wheelchair, and met us on a custom converted tricycle, with a cooler on the back. We all wandered into the backyard, where he had 75 trees, most of which he'd planted about 20 years before. About a third of the orchard was russets (Zabergau Reinette, Roxbury Russet, Golden Russet) and the rest heirlooms like Baldwin or English varieties like Cox's Orange Pippin—"The preferred eating apple in England," Hoover said. He pointed out one tree, full of tiny yellow apples the size of cherries. "This a Golden Hornet crab," he said. I bit into one, and it had crazy, stinging acidity—thus the name. "In the old days you'd add these to Northern Spy or other heirlooms to create tannins."

The Golden Hornet crabs were one of the few trees that had a lot of apples. As we followed Hoover back to his house, Selin told me that biennalism affected his best ciders, too. "I don't make Stone Fence Farm in even years," he said. "And I don't make Packbasket in even years either." That meant neither would be made again until next year.

Inside, Hoover's wife, Peggy Haine, had made a wonderful spread of cheese, hummus, and bread. Selin opened a bottle of his new single-varietal Kingston Black. "It has almost a red wine aroma," said Haine, who is also a journalist. As we sipped, she told a story about attending a conference of water witches or diviners. Hoover eventually opened several of his very good homemade fruit brandies.

Selin opened a bottle of his 2015 Stone Fence Farm, made with apples from right in the backyard. It was a cider of incredible depth, with aromas of mint, eucalyptus, and above all apple peel, along with flavors of ripe apricot, pink grapefruit, and even white pepper. If you served this blind to a wine person, they might guess that this was a grüner veltliner from near the Danube in Austria. But this was completely American. At this point in my journey, I had ceased to worry about using wine language for cider. This cider was so complex, it deserved to be swirled, sniffed, and contemplated. This was true terroir, with historic, heirloom apples cared for and preserved in the same way that Hoover had with the field recordings of traditional Appalachian music.

Sitting there drinking Stone Fence Farm, it struck me again: Cider was nothing new. Cider is not a fad that will "have its moment." Cider is as old as history. But cider is also fragile. Just like that old fiddle and banjo music, cider is complicated and confounding and, if you've never experienced it before, perhaps a little strange. Cider needs people who care deeply about how it's made, and why. Cider needs you.

APPENDIX

TOP CIDER BARS IN AMERICA

The Northman. Chicago, Illinois.
Possibly the most influential cider bar in America, always offering more than two dozen ciders on tap. Selections span the globe, from Michigan to the Basque Country to Oregon to Normandy to New England. Staying on the apple theme, The Northman also has one of the largest selections of Calvados in the world. **thenorthman.com**

Anxo Cidery & Pintxos Bar. Washington, District of Columbia.
The cider epicenter of the nation's capital, with two locations. Besides its own fine ciders, the Basque-themed Anxo always offers a well-curated selection of ciders from standouts like Eve's, and it was even named one of "America's Best 100 Wine Restaurants" by *Wine Enthusiast*. **anxodc.com**

Würstbar. Jersey City, New Jersey.
Along with an emphasis on beer and sausages, the breadth of cider on the menu at this gastropub (across the river from Manhattan) is outstanding. Würstbar has dozens of hard-to-find bottles and a draft list that includes a house collaboration with Finger Lakes favorite South Hill. **wurstbarjc.com**

Redfield Cider Bar & Bottle Shop. Oakland, California.
Opened in 2019 by Olivia Maki and Mike Reis, who co-host the cider podcast *Redfield Radio*. This exciting spot caused the *San Francisco Chronicle* to ask: "Can Redfield finally make cider happen in the Bay Area?" **redfieldcider.com**

Finger Lakes Cider House. Interlaken, New York.
This is the cider hub of New York's Finger Lakes, with a great vibe and stunning views of Cayuga Lake. You can sample ciders from Kite &

String (the house brand) as well as guest selections from other local cideries. **fingerlakesciderhouse.com**

Capitol Cider. Seattle, Washington.
This classic bar in Seattle's Capitol Hill neighborhood has one of the nation's largest offerings of cider, with 20 on tap and more than 150 bottles from around the world. **capitolcider.com**

Brooklyn Cider House. Brooklyn, New York.
Beyond their own ciders, made in the Hudson Valley, this bustling bar in Bushwick has 10 ciders on tap and 20 by the bottle from around New York (particularly the Finger Lakes), France, Spain, and New England. **brooklynciderhouse.com**

Schilling Cider House. Portland, Oregon, and Seattle, Washington.
At each of its two locations, Schilling Cider House boasts one of the largest selections of cider on tap in the US. Important stops on the Pacific Northwest's cider trail. **schillingciderhouse.com**

Mullers Cider House. Rochester, New York.
Opened in 2015 making Mullers one of the more venerable cider bars in the nation. Its proximity to the Finger Lakes (a little over half an hour away) means lots of local ciders on the menu. **mullersciderhouse.com**

The Northern Spy. Durham, North Carolina.
The beloved Black Twig Cider House, host of the annual Txotxfest, was acquired in early 2019 by Colorado's Stem Ciders (**stemciders .com**). At the time of this book's publication, they plan to reopen as The Northern Spy—a very exciting development in the world of cider. **northernspync.com**

NOTABLE AMERICAN CIDERIES

NEW YORK

Though New York is the second-largest apple producing state in the US, it is by far the nation's most significant and innovative cider-making area. From Angry Orchard, the 800-pound gorilla of the cider industry, to smaller producers that forage the state's abundant wild apples, a visit to the Finger Lakes and the Hudson Valley is a must for any true cider enthusiast. Check out **newyorkciderassociation.com** for more info.

FINGER LAKES
The Finger Lakes, particularly the isthmus between Seneca Lake and Cayuga Lake, is the most important cider region in the US, with a burgeoning trail of small artisan producers whose focus is on growing cider apples.

Eve's Cidery
evescidery.com

Kite & String Cider
fingerlakesciderhouse.com

Redbyrd Orchard Cider
redbyrdorchardcider.com

Black Diamond Cider
blackdiamondcider.com

South Hill Cider
southhillcider.com

Lake Drum Brewing Star Cider
starcidery.com

Blackduck Cidery
blackduckcidery.com

Bellwether Hard Cider
cidery.com

LAKE ONTARIO
North of the Finger Lakes lies Wayne County and New York's prime commercial orchards. So it stands to reason that good cider can also be found along one of North America's Great Lakes.

Embark Craft Ciderworks
embarkcraftciderworks.com

Blue Barn Cidery
bluebarncidery.com

Rootstock Ciderworks
rootstockciderworks.com

HUDSON VALLEY & THE CATSKILLS
Only a little over an hour from New York City, this region boasts more than 30 cider makers—from craft producers like Sündstrom to Angry Orchard's Innovation Cider House. Check out **hvciderguide.com** for more info.

Angry Orchard
angryorchard.com

Sundström Cider
sundstromcider.com

Aaron Burr Cider
aaronburrcider.com

Metal House Cider
metalhousecider.com

Orchard Hill Cider
orchardhillcidermill.com

Graft Cider
graftcidery.com

Treasury Cider
treasurycider.com

Slyboro Cider
slyboro.com

NEW ENGLAND

New England's apple orchards are iconic, and its cider tradition dates back to the earliest colonial days. New Hampshire, Vermont, and Massachusetts have some of the largest concentration of heritage cider makers. From pioneering orchards like Farnum Hill and West County, which are credited with kickstarting the cider revival in the 1980s, to the extraordinary ice ciders from Eden to new-wave producers like Shacksbury and Citizen Cider, New England is another must-visit for the cider lover.

NEW HAMPSHIRE
Farnum Hill
povertylaneorchards.com

VERMONT
Shacksbury Cider
shacksbury.com

Fable Farm Fermentory
fablefarmfermentory.com

Eden Specialty Ciders
edenciders.com

Citizen Cider
citizencider.com

Tin Hat Cider
tinhatcider.com

Stowe Cider
stowecider.com

Flag Hill Farm
flaghillfarm.com

MASSACHUSETTS
West County Cider
westcountycider.com

Stormalong
stormalong.com

Carr's Ciderhouse
carrsciderhouse.com

Ragged Hill Cider Company
raggedhillcider.com

Far From The Tree
farfromthetreecider.com

MAINE

Cornish Cider Company
cornishcidercompany.com

Urban Farm Fermentory
fermentory.com

MID-ATLANTIC

Virginia, Pennsylvania, and New Jersey all have apple and cider traditions that date back to early America. Newly planted cider orchards, as well as innovative urban cideries—in Washington, Philadelphia, and other cities—make the region an essential part of the nation's cider revival.

VIRGINIA

Too often forgotten in the Northeast-versus-Northwest cider debates, Virgina cider dates back to the days of Thomas Jefferson. To this day, the state (the nation's 5th largest apple grower) still produces excellent cider, from pioneering orchard Foggy Ridge to the heritage ciders of Albemarle County to the urban cidery Blue Bee in Richmond. Check out **virginiacider.org** for more info.

Foggy Ridge
foggyridgecider.com

Potter's Craft Cider
potterscraftcider.com

Albemarle Ciderworks
albemarleciderworks.com

Blue Bee Cidery
bluebeecider.com

Castle Hill
castlehillcider.com

Winchester Ciderworks
winchesterciderworks.com

DISTRICT OF COLUMBIA
Anxo Cidery
anxodc.com

NEW JERSEY
Ironbound
jerseyciderworks.com

PENNSYLVANIA
Hale & True Cider Co.
haleandtrue.com

Kurant Cider
kurantcider.com

WEST VIRGINIA
Hawk Knob
hawkknob.com

MIDWEST

The heart of Midwest apple country is Michigan's Fruit Ridge, in the western part of the state near Grand Rapids, and there is also a robust cider production farther north on the Leelanau Peninsula, near Traverse City. There are also pockets of cider production throughout Minnesota and Wisconsin. Virtue Cider, based near Grand Rapids and now owned by Anheuser-Busch InBev, and JK's Farmhouse Ciders are the two regional powerhouses.

MICHIGAN, NEAR GRAND RAPIDS

Schaefer Cider
schaeferciders.com

The People's Cider
thepeoplescider.com

Vander Mill Cider
vandermill.com

Ridge Cider Co.
ridgecider.com

Uncle John's Cider Mill
ujcidermill.com

MICHIGAN, LEELANAU PENINSULA & TRAVERSE CITY

Tandem Ciders
tandemciders.com

Left Foot Charley
leftfootcharley.com

45 North
fortyfivenorth.com/ciders/

MINNESOTA

Milk & Honey Ciders
milkandhoneyciders.com

Keepsake Cidery
mncider.com

WISCONSIN

ÆppelTreow
aeppeltreow.com

PACIFIC NORTHWEST

Washington is the nation's largest grower of apples, and many consider Portland, Oregon, to be one of the top cider cities in America.

Any serious cider tour must include both. While much of the cider produced in the Pacific Northwest uses culinary fruit and would fall into the USACM's "modern" category, there are a handful of producers making heritage cider.

OREGON

Art + Science, Cider + Wine
artandsciencenw.com

2 Towns Ciderhouse
2townsciderhouse.com

Wandering Aengus Ciderworks
wanderingaengus.com

E.Z. Orchards
ezorchards.com

Bauman's Cider Company
baumanscider.com

WASHINGTON

Snowdrift Cider Co.
snowdriftcider.com

Alpenfire Cider
alpenfirecider.com

Finnriver Farm & Cidery
finnriver.com

CALIFORNIA

While California has the second-most cideries in the US (behind New York), most produce modern rather than heritage ciders. There are, however, a number of producers committed to sourcing cider apples—the most notable being Tilted Shed in Sonoma County, in the midst of wine country.

Tilted Shed
tiltedshed.com

Troy Cider

Wrangletown Cider Company
wrangletowncidercompany.com

Santa Cruz Cider Company
santacruzciderco.com

NOTABLE IMPORTED CIDERS

NORMANDY

Christian Drouin
calvados-drouin.com

Famille Dupont
calvados-dupont.com

Eric Bordelet
ericbordelet.com

Claque-Pépin
claque-pepin.fr

BRITTANY

Manoir du Kinkiz
cidre-kinkiz.fr

Le Brun
cidrelebrun.com

BASQUE SPAIN

Petritegi
petritegi.com

Bereziartua
bereziartuasagardoa.com

Astarbe
astarbe.eus/en/cider

Gurutzeta
gurutzeta.com

Isastegi
isastegi.com

ASTURIAS

Trabanco
sidratrabanco.com

Viuda de Angelón
sidraviudaangelonpomar.es

Riestra
sidrariestra.com

UNITED KINGDOM

Oliver's Cider & Perry
oliversciderandperry.co.uk

Hogan's Cider
hoganscider.co.uk

Ross on Wye Cider & Perry
rosscider.com

Aspall Cyder
aspall.co.uk

GERMANY

Weidmann & Groh
weidmann-groh.de

SWITZERLAND

Ciderie du Vulcain
cidrelevulcain.ch

INDEX